Optimise

Workbook with answer key

B1+

macmillan education

Macmillan Education
4 Crinan Street
London N1 9XW
A division of Macmillan Publishers Limited

Companies and representatives throughout the world

ISBN 978-0-230-48864-9

Written by Angela Bandis and Patricia Reilly

First published 2017

Designed by Ken Vail Graphic Design
Cover design by Designers Collective
Cover photograph by by **Getty Images**/Lisa Gagne; **Shutterstock**/mexrix(background)
Picture research by Emily Taylor

The author and publishers would like to thank the following for permission to reproduce their photographs:
Alamy/Blend Images p40, Alamy/Gareth Byrne p117(bl), Alamy/Corbis Premium RF p88(bl), Alamy/Cultura Creative (RF) p85(br), Alamy/Randy Duchaine p29(bl), Alamy/ES Imagery p78, Alamy/Ikon Images p84, Alamy/Image Source p13(tr), Alamy/David Levenson p85(bl), Alamy/MITO images p45(cr), Alamy/Wiliam Perry p62, Alamy/PhotoAlto p17(tr), Alamy/WENN Ltd p27, Alamy/World History Archive p97; **BananaStock** p95; **Corbis** p49(tr); **Fotolibra** p45(bl); **Getty Images**/Ash Lindsey Photography p16(bl), Getty Images/Alex Belomlinsky p4, Getty Images/Blend Images p109(b,d), Getty Images/Brand X p73(tl), Getty Images/Shaun Curry/AFP p91, Getty Images/Digital Vision p21(tl), Getty Images/Martine Doucet p54, Getty Images/EyeEm p117(br), Getty Images/Lars Forsstedt p14, Getty Images/Hemera/Thinkstock Images p72, Getty Images/David Hills p21(br), Getty Images/iStockphoto/Thinkstock Images p35, Getty Images/iStockphoto/Swisshippo p67, Getty Images/Jose Luis Pelaez Inc/Blend Images LLC p89(tl), Getty Images/Kali Nine LLC p38, Getty Images/Lisa Kimberly p45(tl), Getty Images/Glyn Kirk/AFP p80, Getty Images/Josef Lindau/Corbis/VCG p76, Getty Images/Ryan McVay p117(tr), Getty Images/OJO Images p59, Getty Images/Pagadesign p93, Getty Images/John Phillips p17(br), Getty Images/Photolibrary p109(c), Getty Images/Mike Powell p117(tl), Getty Images/Purestock/Punchstock p13(bottom), Getty Images/Lew Robertson/Fuse p47, Getty Images/Rolfo p109(a), Getty Images/Sylvain Sonnet p29(br), Getty Images/Jamie Squire p79, Getty Images/STR/AFP p77, Getty Images/Vgajic p22, Getty Images/Yellow Dog Productions p29(tl), Getty Images/Yagi Studio p88(br); **Kobal**/Warner BROS TV p26; **PhotoDisc**/Getty Images p81, PhotoDisc/Ryan McVay p17(cr); **Plain Picture**/Kniel Synnatzschke p21(tr); **Rex Features**/Shutterstock/Canadian Press p69(tm), Rex Features/Shutterstock/Everett p65, Rex Features/Shutterstock/Image Source p89(tr), Rex Features/Shutterstock/Music Pics p69(br), Rex Features/Shutterstock/OJO Images p41, Rex Features/Shutterstock/Walt Disney Co p83; **Shutterstock** p36, Shutterstock/Poprotskiy Alexey p61(tm), Shutterstck/Alliance p49(tl), Shutterstock/Andi Berger p8, Shutterstock/Fabio Berti p25, Shutterstock/Fastfun23 p9, Shutterstock/FineShine p30, Shutterstock/Goodluz pp16(br), 29(tr), Shutterstock/Halfpoint p75, Shutterstock/Kaisorn p37, Shutterstock/Koosen p50(clock), Shutterstock/Annamaria Kopacz p52, Shutterstock/Kzenon p73(tr), Shutterstock/lightpoet p42, Shutterstock/Mexitographer p99, Shutterstock/Monkey Business Images p68, Shutterstock/Peter O'Toole p50(drink), Shutterstock/Patjo p61(bm), Shutterstock/Kseniia Perminova p57, Shutterstock/Rawpixel.com p5, Shutterstock/Syda Productions p53, Shutterstock/Tanewpix p20, Shutterstock/Haris Vythoulkas p32, Shutterstock/Westend61 Premium p11, Shutterstock/www.BillionPhotos.com p48, Shutterstock/YanLev p19.

Printed and bound in Uruguay

2023
13

B1+

Contents

Angela Bandis and Patricia Reilly

macmillan education

1 Can't live without it

READING | Multiple choice

→Student's Book, pages 4–5

1 Read the article opposite then write the correct letter (A–F) to complete the descriptions.

1 In paragraph ____ the writer wants us to think about technology use on vacation.
2 In paragraph ____ the writer describes ways of cutting down technology use at home.
3 In paragraph ____ the writer talks about the amount of time people spend using technology.
4 In paragraph ____ the writer gives examples of increasing opportunities to reduce technology use.
5 In paragraph ____ the writer describes the positive aspects of reducing technology use.
6 In paragraph ____ the writer outlines the negative consequences of using technology too much.

2 Read the article again. For questions 1–5, choose the answer (A, B, C or D) which you think fits best according to the text.

1 What is the writer's purpose in the first paragraph?
- **A** To show that people use many different electronic gadgets.
- **B** To explain that people rarely disconnect from technology.
- **C** To criticise people who use more than one media device.
- **D** To advise people how to safely unplug electronic devices.

2 What is the writer's purpose in the second paragraph?
- **A** To help us understand the harmful effects of too much technology.
- **B** To make us realise that technology doesn't affect everyone.
- **C** To show that modern lifestyles are usually unhealthy.
- **D** To make us realise that technology is good for us.

3 According to the writer,
- **A** it is important to stop using technology altogether.
- **B** you should go for a walk in nature every day.
- **C** reducing your digital contact time a little can help a lot.
- **D** the best thing is to turn off your phone for a while every day.

4 If you really want to digitally detox,
- **A** you should always use the 'quiet carriage' on trains.
- **B** the restaurant in Los Angeles is your best option.
- **C** you should switch off your phone when you go shopping.
- **D** you can go on a holiday without technology.

5 What is the writer's purpose in the final paragraph?
- **A** To persuade us not to buy so many technological gadgets.
- **B** To suggest that everyone will have fun if they don't use technology.
- **C** To show that there are advantages to cutting down on technology use.
- **D** To explain that you will have more friends if you use less technology.

3 Find these words or phrases in the article. Then match them to the definitions below.

attention span | bombardment | clarity of mind | eatery | life coach | retreat | tech dependence | unplug

1 separate a piece of equipment from a power supply (paragraph A) ______
2 a situation where someone gets a lot of things to deal with (paragraph A) ______
3 a situation where you need technology to live or succeed (paragraph B) ______
4 the time you can spend concentrating (paragraph B) ______
5 to avoid a dangerous or unpleasant situation by moving away from it (paragraph D) ______
6 a place where you can have a meal (paragraph D) ______
7 someone who gives advice to people who want to improve their lives (paragraph E) ______
8 the ability to think clearly or understand things clearly (paragraph F) ______

A How much time do you spend every day using technology? The shocking results of a study in the UK show that people living there now spend more time each day using media devices, such as laptops, mobile phones and tablets, than they do sleeping! Another study showed that 53% of young people never switch off completely from all personal technology and only 6% manage to totally unplug once a week. We live in a world where technology is everywhere 24/7 and we find it hard to disconnect from this digital bombardment.

B Increasingly, experts are recommending a digital detox – spending time without technology – to combat the negative effects of tech dependence. Spending hours using technology every day can have a serious physical and emotional impact. While some people may only feel a little anxious when they cannot access their devices, for others the risks are more significant. Technology overuse has been linked to obesity, a poor attention span, an increase in stress and anxiety, poor sleep and low energy levels.

C If the idea of disconnecting from media devices fills you with horror, you are not alone. However, it needn't mean totally cutting yourself off from technology. Small changes to your lifestyle can make a big difference – for example, create a technology-free zone at home, unplug for just one hour a day, ideally the hour before you go to sleep. Experiment with going out without your phone, and spend a minimum of 30 minutes in nature, electronic-free, at least once a week.

D Outside the home, there is growing recognition of the need for breaks from technology. Many UK trains now have 'quiet carriages' where mobile phones cannot be used. In Amsterdam, people are being encouraged to use the city's 'No Wi-Fi' benches, which block wi-fi signals. A famous London department store recently opened a phone-free 'silence room' for shoppers to retreat to, and *Eva Restaurant* in Los Angeles has just become the first eatery to offer a discount if you leave your phone in reception.

E Those that want to go a step further can now book a digital detox holiday. There are an increasing number of travel companies which offer different 'de-tech' packages, ranging from places that are wi-fi free to hotels where you have to hand over all your electronic devices when you check in. Some packages even include sessions with a life coach to give advice on how to use your tech-free time productively!

F There are important benefits to digitally detoxing, which include better concentration, increased creativity and clarity of mind, improved social relationships and reduced stress and anxiety. So what are you waiting for? Switch off now – you never know, you might even enjoy it!

1 GRAMMAR 1 | Tense review: present simple and continuous, stative verbs

→Student's Book, page 6 →Grammar reference, Unit 1, Student's Book, page 148

1 Choose the correct answers.

1 Rosie's parents are buying a new 3D TV.
a) No, they don't.
b) No, they're not.

2 Mum, do you know where George is?
a) I think he watches TV.
b) I think he's watching TV.

3 Where does your brother work?
a) He's working at an internet café for now.
b) He works at an internet café for now.

4 Are you on the internet much?
a) No, I don't go online a lot.
b) No, I'm not going online a lot.

5 Lots of people are into Twitter these days.
a) Yes, it becomes more and more popular.
b) Yes, it's becoming more and more popular.

6 How do smartphones work?
a) They use digital technology.
b) They're using digital technology.

2 Choose the correct words.

About Me | Contact | Blog | Photo Albums ▾

ZACK SPEAKS THE TRUTH

Today's topic: Do you really need a new phone?

Whenever I (**1**) **tell / am telling** my friends how old my phone is, they (**2**) **think / are thinking** that I (**3**) **joke / am joking**. I'm not, though. I got this phone three years ago. I can still upload my photos and keep up to date with social media. All of the apps I have still (**4**) **work / are working**. In other words, there is nothing wrong with it.
My friend Max, on the other hand, only got a new mobile phone last year and already he (**5**) **thinks / is thinking** about upgrading. But it's not because it's broken. Max is like a lot of my friends – they (**6**) **see / are seeing** ads for the latest phones and they (**7**) **feel / are feeling** the pressure to buy them. After all, the people in the ads are usually cool and (**8**) **look / are looking** like they (**9**) **have / are having** a great time. The message is that 'new tech' means 'cool'. Well, I definitely (**10**) **don't think / am not thinking** so!

3 Complete the sentences with the correct form of the verbs in brackets. Use the present simple or continuous.

1 Grandpa ____________ to the radio; he's asleep in his chair. (**not listen**)
2 Mark ____________ quite a few hours a day on Facebook and Twitter. (**spend**)
3 The boys aren't here. They ____________ the football final on Jack's wide-screen TV. (**watch**)
4 This satnav system is useless; it only ____________ some of the time. (**work**)
5 My brother ____________ my laptop and it's really annoying! (**always / borrow**)
6 ____________ a Samsung or an iPhone? Have you decided yet? (**you / buy**)
7 The tablet I bought on eBay isn't great; it ____________ videos very well. (**not stream**)
8 This video ____________ ages to download. It's been 30 minutes already. (**take**)

1 VOCABULARY | Word formation | Collocations | Topic vocabulary

→Student's Book, page 7 →Vocabulary reference, Student's Book, page 162

1 Complete the sentences with the adjective form of the word in brackets.

1 It's ________ (**admire**) that some businesses are providing local schools with computers for free.
2 If you watch too much bad TV, you'll become stupid, and I don't think stupidity is ________ (**reverse**)!
3 The technician couldn't fix our laptop because he couldn't find an ________ (**identify**) cause of the problem.
4 It's a very popular online newspaper, but some of the stories aren't ________ (**believe**).
5 When the ________ (**terror**) accident occurred, Twitter users were the first to report it.
6 There should be controls on some online sites so that they are not ________ (**access**) to young children.
7 I don't care about being ________ (**fashion**), so I'm not going to change my phone for the latest model.
8 Is it ________ (**permit**) for people under the age of 18 to join social network sites?
9 Don't watch videos! You should be studying – that's the ________ (**sense**) thing to do.
10 A ________ (**horror**) thing happened to Darcy last night – she had no internet, so she couldn't go on Facebook!
11 I spend an hour a day online, and I think that's ________ (**reason**), don't you?
12 Video games are really fun, but it's ________ (**advice**) not to become addicted to them.

2 Complete the dialogues with the collocations in the box in the correct form.

come to an agreement | come to the decision do me a favour | do my best | make progress take my advice | take your point

1 **A:** Hmm ... the Samsung or the iPhone? What do you think?

B: ______________________ and save your money. There's nothing wrong with your old phone.

2 **A:** Can you ______________________ ? Can you show me how to use my new tablet?

B: Of course I can. It's really easy.

3 **A:** Are you ______________________ with your science project?

B: Yes, I am. Amy's helping me with it and it's going very well.

4 **A:** Last night I ______________________ that we need to spend more time together as a family.

B: Does that mean I can't watch DVDs in my room after school, Dad?

5 **A:** I think technology can be very harmful.

B: I ______________________ , but I'd rather have it than not have it.

6 **A:** It's a difficult exam. Do you think you'll pass?

B: Well, I'll ______________________ and hopefully that will be enough.

7 **A:** So, have we ______________________ ? Are you OK to share your computer with your sister?

B: No, I'm not. I don't want to share it with anyone!

3 Choose the correct words to complete the text.

1	Use of mobile phones is **limited** / **mended** to break time and lunchtime.
2	All students must **post** / **switch** off their phones at the beginning of each lesson.
3	Students who want to **go** / **turn** online can use the computers in the library.
4	Please **turn** / **mend** off all computers at the end of the day.
5	You mustn't **upload** / **fix** photos taken at school to any social networking site on the **line** / **internet**.
6	If you have a problem with a school computer, call the school engineer. Do not try and **fix** / **limit** the problem yourself.
7	Do not use broken or damaged equipment. Wait until it has been **switched** / **repaired**.
8	Please do not bring expensive **repairs** / **gadgets** into school. You are responsible for them if they break.
9	You can **post** / **limit** positive comments about teachers and students on our school's **online** / **upload** forum.

1 GRAMMAR 2 | *-ing* and infinitives

→ Student's Book, page 9 → Grammar reference, Unit 1, Student's Book, page 148

1 Choose the correct words.

1 **A:** You've got a nice phone. I hope **buy** / **to buy** the same model as soon as I can afford it.

B: To be honest, I can't help **to think** / **thinking** I wasted my money. There are cheaper phones that are just as good.

2 **A:** You always seem **being** / **to be** at your computer. Don't you have any hobbies outside of the house?

B: Well, I'm interested in **to play** / **playing** football, though I'm not very good at it. But with a computer game, I can be a champion!

3 **A:** Joe, did you forget **to charge** / **charging** the tablet again? It's dead.

B: No, I remember **to do** / **doing** it yesterday. Maybe there's a problem with the battery.

4 **A:** I'd rather you **didn't use** / **not to use** my laptop without asking me first.

B: But I needed to find some information online and Mum said it was OK. She lets me **use** / **to use** it all the time.

5 **A:** My parents encouraged me **studying** / **to study** computer programming, and I did.

B: Do you regret **to do** / **doing** that now, or are you happy with your career?

2 Match to make sentences. Use the words in italics to help you.

1 I *prefer* ____
2 I *stopped* ____
3 I'm *beginning* ____
4 I *noticed* ____
5 I *don't mind* ____
6 I *refuse* ____

a) *paying* a bit more for a top quality phone.
b) *to understand* how gaming can become addictive.
c) *to spend* a lot of money on a gadget.
d) *using* a laptop to surfing the net on a tablet.
e) *him taking* a photo on his mobile phone.
f) *playing* the game and watched TV instead.

1 LISTENING | Multiple choice (extracts)

→ Student's Book, page 8

1 01 **Listen to the comments and choose the sentence (a or b) that best summarises what the speaker says.**

1 **a)** I don't want to disagree with you.
b) You have to agree with me.

2 **a)** We can't agree, but that's OK.
b) It's good that we agree.

3 **a)** I strongly disagree with you.
b) I agree with you 100%.

4 **a)** There is no way that I can agree with you.
b) I know that you are not being serious.

5 **a)** That's exactly how I feel.
b) I'm not sure I agree with you.

2 02 **You will hear people talking in five different situations. For each question, choose the best answer (A, B or C).**

1 You hear a young man and a young woman talking. What do they disagree about?
A how expensive the latest phones are
B the importance of having an up-to-date phone
C what the young man spends his money on

2 You hear a man and a woman talking. What do they agree to do?
A accept each other's opinion
B buy a new television set
C discuss the problem again

3 You hear a man and a girl talking. What do they agree about?
A The technician was not right.
B He will give the girl back her money.
C It's wrong that the tablet is still broken.

4 You hear two women talking. What do they agree about?
A a parent's role in children's screen time
B how much a parent can trust a child
C how responsible children can be

5 You hear a father and son talking. What do they disagree about?
A that the boy bought another video game
B that the boy bought a specific video game
C that the boy bought the game to be cool

1 SPEAKING | Interview

→ Student's Book, page 10

1 Complete the sentences with the words in the box.

a | ever | in | never | now | tend | time | typical | up | usual

1 A ____________ Saturday for me is to go out for the afternoon with my friends. We usually go shopping or hang out at a café. Sunday is a lazy day. I ____________ to see my friends if I can, but I rarely go out on Sunday night because I have to get up early the next day for school.

2 I love reading in bed, and I often spend ____________ to an hour ____________ day reading before I finally go to sleep. Recently I finished reading *The Fault in Our Stars* by John Green, which I thought was excellent.

3 My ____________ routine is to relax for about half an hour. From time to ____________ I cook dinner because I love cooking, but usually it's my mum who does it. After dinner, I play video games or surf the internet. I hardly ____________ go out during the week because I've got homework to finish, and where I live there's really nothing to do ____________ the evening.

4 Yes, I do, but I only do them at the weekend. I ____________ have any free time on weeknights because I am too busy with school work. However, on Saturdays I play in a band with some friends; I'm the bass player.

5 During the week, yes. We have dinner and watch TV together almost every evening. But at the weekends, I like spending time with friends. Every ____________ and again we do something as a family, though.

2 Match paragraphs 1–5 in Exercise 1 to questions a–e.

____ **a)** What do you do after school?
____ **b)** How much time do you spend reading?
____ **c)** What do you like doing at the weekend?
____ **d)** Do you spend a lot of time with your family?
____ **e)** Do you have any hobbies?

3 **Write your own answers to the questions in Exercise 2.**

1 ______________________________

2 ______________________________

3 ______________________________

4 ______________________________

5 ______________________________

1 USE OF ENGLISH | Sentence transformation

→Student's Book, page 11

1 **Complete the table with the words and phrases in the box. Some words and phrases can be used more than once.**

~~agree~~ | be good at | make | mind | remember (× 2) | see | tend | would like

1) verb + (object) + full infinitive	2) verb + (object) + -*ing*	3) verb + object + bare infinitive
agree		

2 **Choose the correct sentence endings. Use the words in italics to help you. Sometimes more than one answer is correct.**

1 You should be preparing for your final exams *instead of*
a) surf the internet. **b)** to surf the internet.
c) surfing the internet.

2 I've got a new laptop and Carl *offered*
a) set it up for me. **b)** to set it up for me.
c) setting it up for me.

3 Don't *risk*
a) your health. **b)** to harm your health.
c) harming your health.

4 You could *pretend*
a) being unwell. **b)** to be unwell.
c) be unwell.

5 He played the game all day, but he *stopped*
a) playing to have dinner. **b)** to have dinner.
c) play for dinner.

6 It was late but David *carried on*
a) chat online. **b)** to chat online.
c) chatting online.

7 Of all the computers here, I *would prefer*
a) buying this one. **b)** this one.
c) to buy this one.

8 I *love*
a) taking selfies. **b)** to take selfies.
c) take selfies.

3 **Complete the second sentence so it has a similar meaning to the first. Do not change the word given. Use two to five words, including the word given.**

1 Mia can work out technical problems; she has a talent for it. **GOOD**
Mia's ______________________ technical problems.

2 Tom and Zak came to an agreement about sharing the laptop. **AGREED**
Tom and Zak ______________________ the laptop.

3 Will you let me go to the digital seminar, Dad? **MIND**
Do you ______________________ to the digital seminar, Dad?

4 I don't recall if I turned off the TV last night. **REMEMBER**
I ______________________ the TV last night.

5 Jen's busy and she doesn't usually waste time online. **TENDS**
Jen's busy so she ______________________ time online.

6 It's my mum's fault that I dropped my phone. **MADE**
My mum ______________________ my phone.

1 WRITING | An essay

→Student's Book, pages 12–13 →Writing reference, Student's Book, page 174

1 Choose the correct words to complete the exam skill advice.

1 When you are writing, you **might** / **never** need to agree or disagree with ideas.

2 Try to use a range of **phrases** / **words** that refer to ideas, such as, *I am against the idea that …* or *I disagree with the argument that …*

2 Read the exam task below. Then write A–D in the paragraph plan to put the paragraphs in the correct order.

Paragraph 1	introduction to the subject	___
Paragraph 2	first point that agrees with the statement	___
Paragraph 3	second point that agrees with the statement	___
Paragraph 4	conclusion/summary of opinion	___

Teenagers should spend less time using technology to communicate and more time communicating face-to-face.
Do you agree?

A *Teenagers who spend too much time communicating with other people through a screen rather than in person can struggle to connect emotionally. I completely support the idea that this can make it harder for them to develop close relationships with 'real' people and can make them feel isolated.*

B *Of course, technology can be useful to communicate sometimes. I am not in favour of teenagers never using it at all. However, I think teenagers would benefit from spending more time interacting face-to-face and less time communicating through screens.*

C *Today, it is very common for young people to use technology to communicate. Even when teenagers are with their friends, they are often on their phones rather than actually talking to each other. I totally agree with the idea that teenagers should spend more time communicating face-to-face.*

D *In addition, I do not accept the idea that it's important to be digitally 'connected' with your friends 24/7. Sending more text messages does not mean you are closer to someone. In my opinion, it is better to spend half an hour being with someone rather than texting them.*

3 Rearrange the letters to make words that complete these phrases for agreeing/disagreeing. Then find and underline the phrases in the text.

1 I am not in ___________ of … **avufor**

2 I do not ___________ the idea that … **ceatcp**

3 I ___________ agree with the idea that … **lyatotl**

4 I completely ___________ the idea that … **tropsup**

4 Complete these opinion phrases with your own ideas about teenagers using technology to communicate.

1 It is my belief that *technology improves communication because it means students can communicate with other young people anywhere in the world.*

2 I tend to think that ___________________________.

3 From my point of view, ___________________________.

4 As far as I'm concerned, ___________________________.

PROGRESS CHECK

1 **Choose the correct words.**

1 **A:** That's a strange-looking gadget. What **do you think** / **are you thinking** it is?
B: I have no idea, but I'm trying **working** / **to work** it out.

2 **A:** Lina's on the phone now. She **calls** / **is calling** the computer technician.
B: I hope he is able **to fix** / **fixing** the problem.

3 **A:** Dev, please stop **to surf** / **surfing** the net and do your homework.
B: I'm online because I **do** / **am doing** some research, Mum.

4 **A:** I prefer sending text messages to **make** / **making** phone calls.
B: Me too. It **saves** / **is saving** time and money.

5 **A:** Do you fancy **to go** / **going** to the technology exhibition?
B: I'd like to, but I **study** / **am studying** for a test at the moment.

6 **A:** I heard Oliver **say** / **to say** that he lost his phone.
B: Yes, he lost it yesterday, and he **goes** / **is going** crazy looking for it.

2 **Complete the sentences with the words in the box in the correct form.**

accessible | cause | do (× 2) | fix | gadgets | make | online permissible | reasonable | reversible | switch | take (× 2)

1 I think there's a problem with my phone. I can't hear it when it rings. Could you ____________ me a favour and call me now? I want to check it.

2 I'm getting worried. I haven't ____________ any progress with my technology project for school.

3 Jess bought a cheap charger which ____________ her phone to catch fire. So ____________ my advice – only use approved products with your phone.

4 I ____________ your point about the danger of internet addiction for children, but you can't stop them using digital technology; it wouldn't be ____________ to do that.

5 Is it true that the microwaves from ____________ like mobile phones and tablets can affect the brain and that the damage is not ____________ ?

6 I regularly read an ____________ newspaper, but some of the articles are only ____________ if you have a subscription, and I haven't.

7 I'm so sorry! I dropped your tablet and the screen is broken. I'll ____________ my best to get someone to ____________ it as soon as possible.

8 It isn't ____________ to use your mobile phone in the hospital, so please ____________ it off before you go inside.

Cumulative progress 1 2 3 4 5 6 7 8 9 10 11 12

3 **Choose the correct word or phrase for each gap.**

I own quite a few (**1**) ____________ . They include a smartphone, a laptop, a camera and a tablet. It's hard to pick a favourite, but I suppose if I had to choose, it would be my mobile phone. It combines all of the things that I need (**2**) ____________ daily in one device. Strangely enough though, I hardly (**3**) ____________ make phone calls, but I do send lots of text messages and emails. The phone has an awesome camera, so I take rather a lot of photos with it, which I later (**4**) ____________ to Instagram or post on Facebook. I can't imagine (**5**) ____________ without a mobile phone, but that's due to the fact that I've grown up with this technology. Everyone I know has one, and maybe that's what makes this gadget seem essential. I'm (**6**) ____________ to contact my friends at any time, and we can share photos, music and videos. For me, that's the best thing about mobile phones – they keep you connected with other people.

1	**A** technologies	**B** gadgets	**C** technology	**D** electronics
2	**A** use	**B** to use	**C** be using	**D** using
3	**A** ever	**B** never	**C** much	**D** always
4	**A** mend	**B** repair	**C** switch	**D** upload
5	**A** living	**B** live	**C** to live	**D** to be living
6	**A** ability	**B** able	**C** being able	**D** be able

2 Live and learn

READING | Gapped text

→Student's Book, pages 14–15

1 Read the text opposite and label the paragraphs 1–6 with the headings a–f.

a) Improving your own learning
b) The happiness factor
c) New you
d) Making time
e) Meeting people
f) A sense of achievement

2 Read the sentences and focus on the pronouns in bold. Then answer the questions.

1 ***It** gave **me** a much needed boost in confidence.*
Does **it** probably refer to an experience/event or to a person? ______________________
Does **me** indicate a person talking about themselves or someone else? ______________________

2 ***We** shared ideas and experiences and supported each other.*
Which paragraph(s) refer(s) to people doing something together? ______________________

3 ***This** is especially true for skills that **you** are genuinely interested in.*
If you are 'genuinely interested' in something, is **this** experience generally positive or negative? ______________________
Does **you** refer to one specific person or people in general? ______________________

4 *If you really want to do **them**, you organise your day so you can.*
Does **them** refer to one thing or more than one thing? ______________________

3 Read the text again. Choose from sentences A–G the one which fits each gap 1–6. There is one extra sentence you do not need.

A It gave me a much needed boost in confidence.
B We shared ideas and experiences and supported each other.
C This is especially true for skills that you are genuinely interested in.
D This is the key to being successful and feeling good about yourself.
E You may be able to apply what you learn to other aspects of your life.
F This can often form the basis for long-lasting and satisfying relationships.
G If you really want to do them, you organise your day so you can.

4 Find words or phrases in the text which match these definitions.

1 a variety of things or ideas (paragraph 1) ______________________
2 a difference between two or more ideas, statements, etc. that makes it impossible for both/all of them to be true (paragraph 2) ______________________
3 decide the order to do things, depending on how important or urgent they are (paragraph 2) ______________________
4 learning how to do something well (paragraph 3) ______________________
5 finishing something successfully (paragraph 3) ______________________
6 increases (paragraph 3) ______________________
7 a person who likes to do things on their own (paragraph 5) ______________________
8 getting (paragraph 6) ______________________

Learning new skills

You may be busy learning lots of things at school, but you should seriously think about learning new skills. It turns out that there are a lot of advantages to doing so.

1 ______________________

Studies show that learning new skills increases the body's production of dopamine, the chemical in your brain that makes you feel happy. [1] Try out different things until you find the activities that you feel passionate about. 'Surfing changed my life,' says Liam, 16. 'When I'm out in the water, nothing else matters. I stop worrying about exams and other stuff. I have never felt better.'

2 ______________________

It might sound like a contradiction, but one of the surprising benefits of learning something new is having more free time. With school and homework, many teenagers complain they are too busy for hobbies. However, research shows that adding new activities to your schedule can improve your time management. [2] You find ways to plan and prioritise your activities, which is an important life skill.

3 ______________________

Mastering a new skill also gives you a sense of pride in your achievements. Katy, 17, says, 'When I was first learning to ski, I fell over a lot and considered giving up. Then suddenly everything came together and I did a run without falling once. That was a key moment. [3] It made me feel I could do anything.' Accomplishing something and overcoming fears also boosts your overall confidence and self-esteem.

4 ______________________

When you do a new activity, especially a group activity, you tend to get to know people with similar interests and tastes to your own. It is a great opportunity to make new friends. After all, doing the same activity is sharing a common experience. [4]

5 ______________________

A new skill can open up new learning styles and techniques that can benefit you. 'I tended to be a loner when it came to learning things, but when I took up the guitar, I got nowhere by myself,' says Gracie. 'Then a friend suggested doing practice sessions together. [5] I learnt so much and started to improve. I wish I had tried collaborative learning before.' Sometimes changing your approach to learning can really make the difference. [6]

6 ______________________

Acquiring new skills gives you the chance to experiment with different things. And you never know, you might even find hidden talents or find what you want to do with your life.

2 GRAMMAR 1 | Tense review: past simple and past continuous

→ Student's Book, page 16 → Grammar reference, Unit 2, Student's Book, page 149

1 Choose the correct words.

1 Our teacher was angry because he **saw / was seeing** me sending a text message in class.

2 Ed **was always / was always being** the naughtiest boy in class.

3 Amy looked up. The sun **shone / was shining** brightly in the sky and it made her happy.

4 As the teacher entered the class, some students **talked / were talking** and others **played / were playing** with their phones, so they didn't notice her.

5 'I **do / did do** my homework, but the dog ate it, sir!' said Max to Mr Smith.

6 'Where **did you go / were you going** at nine o'clock this morning when I saw you?'

7 During his life, Leonardo da Vinci **investigated / was investigating** the possibility of human flight.

8 I made that mistake in my essay because I was tired and I **didn't think / wasn't thinking** clearly.

9 We **always went / were always going** camping during the school holidays and had lots of fun.

10 Alicia **went / was going** to the library twice yesterday because she left her phone there the first time.

2 Complete the text with the past simple or past continuous form of the verbs in the box.

bother | fall | find | know | laugh | lie | look forward to not like | prefer | reply | snow | speak | wake up | wonder

It was Thursday night. I was listening to music and my sister Sally **(1)** ___________ in bed, unable to sleep. Something **(2)** ___________ her and I **(3)** ___________ what it was. She was nervous about Sports Day at our school. I **(4)** ___________ it because I was a good runner, but Sally **(5)** ___________ physical activity at all because she **(6)** ___________ it boring. Sally **(7)** ___________ to read books or watch interesting documentaries on TV. I **(8)** ___________ what I could say to make her feel better when Sally suddenly **(9)** ___________. 'It's really cold tonight. Maybe we'll have snow tomorrow,' she said and **(10)** ___________ asleep.

When I **(11)** ___________ the next morning, Sally was at the window and she **(12)** ___________. 'What's so funny?' I asked. 'Look outside,' she **(13)** ___________, and I did. It **(14)** ___________ heavily! Sports Day was cancelled!

2 VOCABULARY | Topic vocabulary | Word formation | Phrasal verbs

→ Student's Book, page 17 → Vocabulary reference, Student's Book, page 162

1 Match to make sentences.

1 This year, Alan managed
2 Jo was delighted when she succeeded
3 England failed
4 We lost
5 Tom came first
6 I can't believe everyone beat
7 Our school has accomplished
8 The mountaineers overcame
9 Anita achieved

a) in passing her music exam.
b) in the final and won the gold medal.
c) a lot in science and sport this year.
d) to run a marathon in under three hours.
e) me and I came last in the test.
f) lots of problems and are now progressing well.
g) her best time of the year in the 10,000 m race.
h) to get to the final of the football World Cup.
i) the match in the last minute of the game.

2 **Complete the dialogues with the correct form (adjective or adverb) of the word in brackets.**

1 **A:** Are you __________ (**ACT**) involved in the art club?
B: Yes, I am and I love it. It gives me the chance to show how __________ (**CREATE**) I am.

2 **A:** You should watch this video. It explains how you can study more __________ (**EFFECT**).
B: Thanks. I need all the help I can get. Exams week is a very __________ (**STRESS**) time!

3 **A:** I enjoyed my first dance lesson, but my feet were very __________ (**PAIN**) for a few days!
B: Well, __________ (**THANK**) you're OK now and can attend the next lesson.

4 **A:** That's a very __________ (**ATTRACT**) mug. Where did you buy it?
B: I didn't. I made it at my pottery class. It's very __________ (**USE**), too.

5 **A:** Is Jack using his time __________ (**PRODUCT**), or is he wasting it playing video games?
B: Leave him alone. What he's doing isn't __________ (**HARM**). He's just enjoying himself during his school holidays.

6 **A:** You're being very __________ (**SECRET**), Jane. What are you hiding in your room?
B: It's a kitten I found in the park, Dad. It's so cute and __________ (**PLAY**). Please can I keep it?

3 **Complete the sentences with the phrasal verbs in the box in the correct form.**

build up | carry out | do without | end up | get on with | get up to | go about | put up with

1 As a teacher, can you tell me how you __________ making students behave?
2 There are no places on the Italian course, so you might __________ learning Spanish.
3 Andy is so disruptive in class that not even his classmates can __________ him.
4 Being patient with shy students can help them to __________ their confidence.
5 'The break has finished, so please __________ your work,' said the teacher.
6 After you __________ the experiment, you must write down your results.
7 During the survival course in the jungle, we had to __________ our phones.
8 How was your school trip to London? What did you __________ in the city?

2 GRAMMAR 2 | *Would, used to, be used to*

→ Student's Book, page 19 → Grammar reference, Unit 2, Student's Book, page 149

1 **Choose the correct option to best summarise each sentence.**

1 I didn't use to like ancient history, but my trip to Greece and Italy changed that.
a) I still don't like ancient history.
b) I like ancient history now.

2 When Grandma was a girl, students would stand up when the teacher entered the classroom.
a) Students stood up every time.
b) Students stood up sometimes.

3 Jade is a teacher and is used to marking lots of homework.
a) She doesn't mark homework now.
b) She is now comfortable with marking homework.

4 I always used to make my own breakfast before school in the morning.
a) This was my habit in the past.
b) I only did this a few times.

5 When it was raining, we would take the bus to school.
a) We always went to school by bus.
b) We sometimes went to school by bus.

2 **Choose the correct words.**

1 **A:** Did you **use / used** to like art at school?
B: Actually, I didn't like it at all!

2 **A:** I'm afraid Alfie doesn't like his new school very much.
B: That's because he isn't **use / used** to it. He'll be fine in a few weeks.

3 **A:** When I was at school, I **wasn't used to / wouldn't** speak rudely to my teachers.
B: Unfortunately, I think things have changed since then.

4 **A:** **Are / Did** you used to the weather in this country?
B: No, and I've been here for five years!

5 **A:** Do you both like teaching in England?
B: Yes, but when we lived abroad, we **were used to / used to** having longer school holidays.

6 **A:** Has Matthew always been in the school band?
B: He **didn't use to / wouldn't** be, but he joined last month.

2 LISTENING | Sentence completion

→ Student's Book, page 18

1 **Look at the sentences below. Choose from the phrases a–d to say what kind of information you think is missing from each one.**

1 He went to ____ during the school holidays.
2 The people in the group thought of themselves as ____ .
3 One of the ways they travelled on the river was by ____ .
4 The group spent ____ there and it was very exciting.

a) a period of time
b) a form of transport
c) a place
d) a descriptive adjective or noun

2 03 **Now listen to the beginning of a talk and write the words that complete the sentences in Exercise 1.**

1 ____________ 2 ____________ 3 ____________ 4 ____________

3 04 **Listen to a teenager called Will talking about a trip to the Amazon rainforest. Complete the sentences with a word or short phrase.**

1 Will's teacher asked him to talk about his ____________ in the Amazon.
2 The cooking facilities at the lodges were ____________ .
3 About ____________ of the Amazon rainforest is found in Brazil.
4 The air in the rainforest was ____________ .
5 Will was annoyed by the ____________ , which were all over the place.
6 Will wasn't expecting to see a ____________ frog.
7 At night, it's possible to step on a ____________ .
8 The bridges are scary because they moved from ____________ .

2 SPEAKING | Photo task

→ Student's Book, page 20

1 **Look at the exam question and the photographs below. Tick the main ideas that are relevant to the question and put a cross next to the ideas which are irrelevant details.**

Compare the photographs and say **which situation you think is more enjoyable**.

1 They show young people in learning situations with adults. ☐
2 One man is wearing a black shirt, but the other is wearing a grey shirt. ☐
3 The skills being learnt in the photos are physical skills. ☐
4 Both the young people are wearing things on their heads. ☐
5 The relationship between the adults and the young people is probably different in each photo. ☐
6 One is happening outside, but the other is happening inside. ☐
7 The sea only appears in one of the photos. ☐
8 The young people are concentrating on what they are doing in both pictures. ☐

2 05 **Look at the photographs again and read the text. Complete the gaps with words for comparing, then listen and check.**

The main (1) ___________ between the pictures is that they (2) ___________ show young people in a learning situation. In the first picture, a child is learning to ride a bike, (3) ___________ in the second picture a girl is learning to make some kind of sweet or pastry. (4) ___________, they both show people who are teaching. However, in the first picture the teacher is a parent, (5) ___________ in the second picture it is a professional. This means the relationship between the teacher and the learner is very different. The pictures also (6) ___________ because one skill is physical, whereas the other one is more practical. Another key (7) ___________ between the pictures is that the first is happening outside while the second is taking place inside. Personally, I think the bike riding situation is (8) ___________ more enjoyable. Maybe it isn't (9) ___________ useful (10) ___________ cooking, but for a young child it represents a big adventure. I think having cooking lessons would be more stressful.

3 **Write four sentences about the photos below, using appropriate words for comparing from Exercise 2.**

1 ___________

2 ___________

3 ___________

4 ___________

2 USE OF ENGLISH | Open cloze

→Student's Book, page 21

1 **Match the grammar forms (a–e) to the words (1–5).**

1 did, has, am ____ a) negative words
2 might, shall, will ____ b) particles
3 not, none, nothing ____ c) modal verbs
4 took, choose, noticed ____ d) main verbs
5 in, on, out ____ e) auxiliary verbs

2 **Look at the sentences. What kind of word completes each gap? Choose from the grammar forms (a–e) in Exercise 1.**

1 It was very late and we had to ___________ going to catch the last bus. ____
2 The teacher asked the class a question, but ___________ knew the answer. ____
3 ___________ you have a favourite teacher when you were at school? ____
4 Most of my classmates were born here and grew ___________ in this area. ____
5 I've got an idea. Maybe we ___________ look for the information we need online. ____

3 **Now complete the sentences in Exercise 2 with one word in each gap.**

4 **Write one word in each gap to complete the text.**

You know him as Wolverine and Van Helsing, but Hugh Jackman wasn't always a Hollywood superstar. In fact, he (1) ___________ had some very unusual and unglamorous jobs! Do you know that he (2) ___________ to be a party clown? It's true. While he (3) ___________ studying at an acting school, he worked as Coco the Clown and he (4) ___________ perform at kids' parties. Unfortunately, he had (5) ___________ tricks to entertain the children, who thought he was a terrible clown. But worse than that was when he dressed up as Kooey the Koala to hand out leaflets for the National Parks and Wildlife Foundation. He had to put up (6) ___________ teenage boys making fun of him, but the heat was also a problem as there were times when he fainted while wearing his costume. On one occasion, he was expected to wear his Kooey costume and run in Sydney's annual 'City To Surf' marathon. So he went down a side street, got into his car and drove to a place near the finishing line. How well (7) ___________ he do? Well, he managed (8) ___________ come 600th out of 40,000 runners and remains the most successful koala in the history of the marathon!

→ Student's Book, pages 22–23 → Writing reference, Student's Book, page 171

1 **Read the exam task and the email that the student wrote and choose T (True) or F (False) for the statements below.**

You have received an email from an English-speaking friend:

> Also, I need your advice. I really want to improve my English, but I'm not sure about the best way to do it. It would be great to do some activities with other people, but I don't know how. I mean, what can I do on my own? Should I just study grammar? What do you think?

Write your **email**.

To: Mario
Subject: Improve your English

Hi Mario,

It was great to hear from you. I'm glad you passed your test, that's brilliant!

You asked me about ways to improve your English. Have you thought about starting an English Club at your school? You could do things like watching films in English together and talking about them, or listening to songs in English. Why not ask your English teacher if you can start one? She might have other ideas about things you can do.

You should also read in English. I know you love comics and art, so what about getting some graphic novels in English? There are some fantastic ones online or I could send you some.

If I were you, I'd practise speaking too. How about Skyping every week? We can chat in English and then you can teach me a bit of Spanish. Another thing you should do is come and stay. If you come during term time, you can come to my school. You'll learn lots of English!

Hope that helps! Let me know if you want to chat online soon!

Cheers!

Sam

1 The exam question is asking for advice. **T / F**
2 This email is written to a friend. **T / F**
3 The first line of the email gives advice. **T / F**
4 The email gives two pieces of advice. **T / F**
5 Each piece of advice has a separate paragraph. **T / F**
6 The email finishes with some natural informal comments. **T / F**

2 **Imagine you have had an email from a friend who wants to go to a two-day pop festival, but whose parents won't let them go. Tick the appropriate advice (1–6).**

1 ☐ Go to the festival without telling your parents.
2 ☐ Ask your friend's parents to talk to your parents.
3 ☐ See if some other friends can come so there is a group of you.
4 ☐ Argue with your parents about it.
5 ☐ Tell your parents that you will call them every day.
6 ☐ Look at the festival website with your parents so they can see you will be safe.

3 **Think of two more good pieces of advice.**

____
____
____
____
____
____

4 **Complete the sentences with ideas from Exercises 2 and 3.**

1 Have you thought about *asking your friend's parents to talk to your parents*?
2 Another thing you might do is ______________________________.
3 Why not ______________________________?
4 If I were you, I'd ______________________________.
5 How about ______________________________?

PROGRESS CHECK

1 Choose the correct words.

Although I laugh about it now, I (1) **wanted / was wanting** to be a lion tamer when I was much younger. I (2) **used to think / would think** it was the most exciting job in the world. In my room, I (3) **was used to / would** put my stuffed toys on the floor and shout instructions at them. I (4) **did / was doing** that one day when my brother (5) **entered / was entering** the room. When he (6) **realised / was realising** what (7) **went on / was going on**, he (8) **started / was starting** laughing uncontrollably. I (9) **didn't use to / wasn't used to** my brother teasing me and I (10) **felt / was feeling** really embarrassed that my secret ambition was no longer secret!

2 Complete the sentences with the verbs in the box in the correct form.

beat | carry | end | fail | get | lose | put | succeed

1 I really enjoy playing chess with my grandad even though I always ___________ to him.
2 In my science class today, I had to ___________ out an experiment with some chemicals, and mine exploded!
3 Greg ___________ to answer any of the questions so didn't pass his exam.
4 Evan always wanted to be an archeologist, but he studied ancient languages instead and ___________ up teaching Latin.
5 The three girls ___________ in building a model plane that could actually fly.
6 Who knows what these students ___________ up to when there are no teachers in the classroom to supervise them!
7 If our class can ___________ all the others in the science competition, we'll win a trip to the Science Museum.
8 You're a primary school teacher, Coral. Tell me, how do you ___________ up with a classroom full of noisy children?

Cumulative progress 1 2 3 4 5 6 7 8 9 10 11 12

3 Write a form of the word in capitals in each gap.

Dyslexia

School was tough for Chris. He had a (1) ___________ time, struggling with reading and spelling. **TERROR** His teachers could find no (2) ___________ cause for this, but the fact remained that Chris was not learning **IDENTIFY** (3) ___________ . **EFFECT**

But (4) ___________ for Chris, a new teacher at his school recognised the signs of dyslexia. **THANK**

Dyslexics often have trouble converting letters to their correct sound, and sounds to their correct letter. This makes traditional learning difficult and very (5) ___________ for them. **STRESS**

The cause of dyslexia is unknown, but we do know that it is a condition which is not (6) ___________ . **REVERSE** It cannot be cured, but it can be overcome with the right kind of learning. The vast majority of dyslexics lead (7) ___________ **PRODUCT** lives, and can often have other 'intellectual' strengths including good problem-solving skills and (8) ___________ thinking. **CREATE**

As for Chris, he got the help he needed and is now doing well at university, where he is studying law and planning a bright future.

3 Viral video

READING | Multiple matching

→Student's Book, pages 26–27

1 Scan the article opposite and write down what these numbers represent.

1 2 __________
2 6 __________
3 10 __________
4 620 __________
5 2014 __________
6 15,000 __________
7 20,000 __________
8 250,000 __________

2 Read the article again. For each question, choose from the people A–D. The people may be chosen more than once.

Which person

1 has to be able to talk to other people in their job? ☐
2 studied for their job using a computer and the internet? ☐
3 has to find information about things in the past? ☐
4 talks about more than one job in film that they have had? ☐
5 gets paid for each day they work? ☐
6 says it's important to be able to find solutions quickly for difficulties? ☐
7 also has another job not related to film? ☐
8 enjoys the fact he/she does many different things as part of the job? ☐

3 Find words and phrases in the article which match these definitions.

1 attractive and interesting in an exciting way (paragraph A) __________
2 the scenery and furniture used in a film to make it look like a particular place (paragraph A) __________
3 subjected to physical or mental stress (paragraph A) __________
4 a talent for any form of art (paragraph B) __________
5 the amount of money that is paid for a certain job (paragraph B) __________
6 type of work (paragraph C) __________
7 the amount of money a person or organisation has to spend on something (paragraph C) __________
8 hard, difficult (paragraph D) __________

www.myworld...

Home | Jobs | Courses | Contacts

The world of film

When most people think about working in film, they think about being an actor, but there are lots of other important roles in the film industry! Here are a few of them you might find interesting.

A I've been a production assistant for six months now. It's not a glamorous job, but I love it because it's so varied – I do all sorts of things in the office, on the set and on location. Yesterday I had to clean the set and tomorrow I might be in the office booking hotels. I started as a runner after I finished school, which was a great opportunity to learn all about production (even if I spent most of my time making cups of tea!). For my job, you have to be organised and good at rapid problem-solving under pressure. My salary is around £15,000, but a senior production assistant can earn £30,000. One day I hope to be a producer – Hollywood here I come! ***Jamie***

B People don't expect to see a woman behind the camera, but that's where you'll find me. I've been a camera operator for four years, which means I prepare and operate the camera and work with the director of photography to achieve the correct visual style for the film. For this job, you should be patient, have artistic ability and be strong (you have to move heavy equipment). No specific qualifications are necessary for the job, but I'd recommend doing a course first – I took a two-year HND (Higher National Diploma) in filmmaking and it helped me enormously. I usually work on a daily rate, which can be anything from £254, on things like news broadcasts, to £620 on big feature films. ***Marina***

C I did a three-year fashion degree and I've worked in my field for over 10 years. I started my current job as a costume designer in 2013 and because I've got a fair bit of experience, my salary is now about £28,000. I'm responsible for designing, creating and getting costumes for all the actors and extras. On my last film, the budget was £20,000, which might sound a lot, but it's soon used up! I manage a team of people and I work with the actors too, so communication skills are really important. You must be good at research too, to make sure the clothes are historically accurate, and you have to have excellent design skills, as well as knowing about fashion and fabrics. ***Katie***

D I've worked freelance as a screenwriter – that's the person who writes the screenplays for films – since 2014. It's a tough field to get into, and I find my work quite tiring as I work part-time in an office too. I've always loved films and writing, so it seemed like the perfect career for me! I did an online writing course, which cost me £349. That gave me a good understanding of how to tell stories, use my imagination and work to tight deadlines – all the things you need for my job. At the moment, I'm working on a sci-fi screenplay, which I hope to sell soon. My hero Michael Arndt sold his screenplay *Little Miss Sunshine* for $250,000 – perhaps I'll make that kind of money one day! ***Stefan***

3 GRAMMAR 1 | Modals (1): review

→ Student's Book, page 28 → Grammar reference, Unit 3, Student's Book, page 150

1 Match the uses of the modals to the sentences.

1 If your video is original, it *might* get a lot of views on YouTube. ____
2 You really *shouldn't* leave such nasty comments online – it's terrible behaviour. ____
3 I *had to* edit the video and add music before it was ready for uploading. ____
4 Sam's website *should* be ready now, so let's go online and check it out. ____
5 We *are allowed to* download these songs because we have paid for them. ____
6 My little brother *could* use a computer when he was only five years old! ____
7 Grandma, you *ought to* get a computer – I think you'd really like it. ____
8 It's illegal to download some movies from the internet, so you *mustn't* do it. ____

a) advice
b) permission
c) criticism
d) obligation
e) ability in the past
f) possibility
g) probability
h) negative obligation (prohibition)

2 Choose the correct words.

1 **A:** You **may not** / **don't have to** buy a new computer.
B: I know. I **can** / **ought** find a good used one on eBay.

2 **A:** **Were you able to** / **Can you** film the concert on your smartphone?
B: Yes, and the video was fine. You **may** / **should** try it when you go to concerts.

3 **A:** You **might** / **ought to** have an anti-virus program on your computer.
B: You're right. **May** / **Could** you recommend one?

4 **A:** **Could** / **Would** you like to go to a video-making seminar with me at the weekend?
B: Sorry, I **can't** / **won't** make it. I'm far too busy this weekend.

5 **A:** You **must** / **may** restart your computer or the program will not work.
B: **Might I** / **Do I have to** do it now or is it OK if I do it later?

6 **A:** Bailey said we **could** / **ought** use his film-editing equipment.
B: Great! **Must** / **Will** he show us how to use it?

3 Complete the blog with the modal verbs in the box.

aren't able to | can | don't have to | had to might | must | should | shouldn't | would

What does it take to go viral?

Posted at 18:00 on 15th December

So you want to be rich and famous, do you? Or maybe just rich? And you're in a hurry, so it (**1**) ____________ happen quickly, right? And you think you (**2**) ____________ definitely make your dreams come true on YouTube. After all, so many others have done it.

Think again! YouTube sensation Felix Kjellberg (**3**) ____________ come up with an original idea that appealed to a young audience. If you (**4**) ____________ develop your own great idea, your channel (**5**) ____________ become like thousands of others on YouTube that have not succeeded.

So here's some advice. You (**6**) ____________ brainstorm to come up with some clever, original ideas. It (**7**) ____________ take you too long to do this. Then talk to your friends about your video ideas and find out which one they (**8**) ____________ be most interested in watching. You (**9**) ____________ take my advice, but if you do, it could make you a star!

3 VOCABULARY | Word formation | Collocations | Topic vocabulary

→ Student's Book, page 29 → Vocabulary reference, Student's Book, page 163

1 Complete the sentences with the noun form of the words in brackets.

1 The singer Sia is known for the ____________ of her music videos. (**original**)
2 It's possible to raise ____________ about environmental issues by making online videos. (**aware**)
3 Are you surprised by the amazing ____________ of Chuggaaconroy? (**popular**)
4 It was the ____________ of her videos that made her an internet sensation. (**clever**)
5 Everyone was charmed by the enthusiasm and ____________ of the boy on the video. (**youthful**)
6 My favourite free-time ____________ is surfing the net and watching videos. (**active**)

7 It gives Mazzi great ____________ to read the many positive comments that people leave on his channel. (**happy**)

8 There's a serious security ____________ on that shopping site, so don't buy anything from there – it's too risky! (**weak**)

9 Despite the ____________ of the editing problem, Amber was able to solve it and upload the video. (**complex**)

10 You should watch this video; it's about the importance of honesty and ____________ in friendships. (**open**)

11 You will be astounded by the ____________ of the young artist in this video. I've never seen anything like it. (**creative**)

12 Playing video games online while talking about them – the ____________ of the idea is genius! (**simple**)

2 **Complete each sentence with two phrases from the box in the correct form.**

do you good | find it funny | go online | have friends round | make fun of | take a break | take part in | tell a joke

1 You look tired. I think it will ____________________ to stop working on your video and ____________________ for a few minutes.

2 I just don't understand people who like to ____________________ others on social media sites or who ____________________ online bullying.

3 My brother has a weird sense of humour. Earlier, he ____________________ he had heard online, but I didn't laugh because I didn't ____________________ at all.

4 At the weekend, I often ____________________ for pizza and then we ____________________ to watch funny videos.

3 **Choose the correct words or phrases.**

1 My favourite **game show / soap opera** is about the lives of people that live on the same street in London.

2 You can learn a lot by watching **documentaries / sitcoms** on TV.

3 Every week the chef explains how to prepare amazing meals on his **cookery show / reality show**.

4 The writers of the **news / sitcom** are brilliant. Every week it's hilarious.

5 We must watch the **weather forecast / wildlife programme** tonight so we know if tomorrow will be sunny.

6 **Chat shows / Reality shows** are only worth watching if the interviewer asks the celebrities interesting questions.

7 Jenny is a great dancer. She should enter one of those **music shows / talent shows** because I think she could win.

8 My dad prefers to read about what is happening around the world rather than watch it on **chat shows / the news**.

3 GRAMMAR 2 | Modals (2): deductions about the present

→ Student's Book, page 31 → Grammar reference, Unit 3, Student's Book, page 151

1 **Match to make sentences.**

1 That can't be Ruby over there ____
2 That might be Ruby over there ____
3 That must be Ruby over there ____

a) so let's stop and say hello to her.
b) because she's away on holiday this week.
c) but it's dark and I can't see very well.

2 **Choose the best modal to complete each sentence.**

1 This ____________ be Caitlyn's channel because her photo is on it and it's called CaitsGr8.
a) can't **b)** might **c)** must

2 I don't know for sure, but this ____________ be the video Harry uploaded yesterday.
a) can't **b)** could **c)** must

3 It says my video has had over a million views, but that ____________ be right as I only uploaded it an hour ago!
a) can't **b)** may **c)** must

4 That ____________ be Joel on the video. I mean, it kind of looks like him, doesn't it?
a) can't **b)** might **c)** must

5 It ____________ be very enjoyable to make comedy videos as a job. I wish I could do it.
a) can't **b)** may **c)** must

6 James spends all of his time watching videos. It ____________ be good for his studies!
a) can't **b)** could **c)** must

3 LISTENING | Multiple matching

→ Student's Book, page 30

1 Which of the sentences below (A–E) are statements of fact (1) and which give an opinion or express an attitude (2)?

A There are a couple of guys whose channels I regularly go to.
B I think it's pretty harmless if it only happens occasionally.
C I never subscribed to any channel online.
D It was really exciting to get viewers' comments.
E It took up too much time, so in the end I just gave up.

1 Statements of fact: ____ , ____
2 Opinions or attitudes: ____ , ____ , ____

2 Match the synonyms to the words and phrases.

1 reassuring ____
2 feel a bit guilty ____
3 appreciate ____
4 encouraging ____
5 exhausting ____
6 hurtful ____

a) makes you feel good and want to continue
b) believe you've done something bad or wrong
c) makes you extremely tired
d) upsetting
e) recognise the value of something
f) comforting

3 06 **You will hear five extracts about online videos. Choose from A–H what each speaker says about them. There are three extra letters you do not need.**

A None of the online channels are worth watching.
B I value the work they've done to make their videos.
C Making the videos was very tiring for me.
D It was easy to record videos with a camera.
E It's comforting to know I can find solutions online.
F I agreed with the negative comments that I read.
G I know it's wrong, but I don't do it often.
H It was nice to get positive feedback, but upsetting if it was negative.

Speaker 1: ☐
Speaker 2: ☐
Speaker 3: ☐
Speaker 4: ☐
Speaker 5: ☐

3 SPEAKING | Collaborative task

→ Student's Book, page 32

1 Tick the five phrases that we use to make suggestions.

1 I'm quite sure … ☐
2 How about … ☐
3 Generally speaking … ☐
4 I suggest we … ☐
5 What about … ☐
6 I agree with you about … ☐
7 One thing we might choose … ☐
8 Why don't we … ☐
9 What's your opinion of … ☐
10 Similarly, … ☐

2 Choose the correct answers.

1 How about ____________ for a subscription?
a) not charge **b)** not charging
c) we not charging

2 What about ____________ it to Facebook?
a) link **b)** to link
c) linking

3 I suggest ____________ a really unusual video.
a) we make **b)** to make
c) we making

4 One thing we might ____________ is having competitions.
a) considering **b)** to consider
c) consider

5 Why don't we ____________ a sports channel?
a) create **b)** to create
c) creating

3 **Imagine you need to think of a way to attract viewers to a new video channel. Match the suggestions (1–5) in Exercise 2 to the justification for them below (a–e).**

a) People love to win prizes. **1** ____
b) So many people are interested in it. **2** ____
c) That would make people notice it. **3** ____
d) People love getting something for nothing. **4** ____
e) That way everyone on our friends list can see it. **5** ____

3 USE OF ENGLISH | Word formation

→ Student's Book, page 33

1 **Choose the correct answers.**

1 Harry is a high ____________, and I'm not surprised his video channel became a hit.
a) achiever **b)** achieve **c)** achievement

2 The ____________ of the match said she was upset by nasty comments left online.
a) lose **b)** loss **c)** loser

3 It must take a lot of talent and ____________ to produce such a beautiful video.
a) creator **b)** creation **c)** creativity

4 The interviewer asked some very ____________ questions, but the star refused to answer.
a) person **b)** personal **c)** personality

5 I'm not surprised she has won awards for the ____________ of her short videos.
a) origin **b)** original **c)** originality

2 **Write a form of the word in capitals in each gap.**

Does your brain hurt?

It has been my (**1**) ____________ for some time now that the internet is making us stupid. This (**2**) ____________ of intelligence is quite worrying. Having access to unlimited information 24/7 is destroying our (**3**) ____________ to think for ourselves. Being able to find addresses, names, events, even what our friends have been up to recently, means we no longer rely on memory. — **BELIEVE**, **LOSE**, **CAPABLE**

We used to be (**4**) ____________, but now we look online for everything. — **THINK**

It gets worse, though, in my opinion. Just look at some of the online video sites.

Given a (**5**) ____________, many people would prefer to watch a cat video than a documentary. It's a (**6**) ____________ that is easily made: Do I want to be entertained or educated? 'Click' on cat video. — **CHOOSE**, **DECIDE**

If you think this (**7**) ____________ of ours for entertainment is not very serious, think again. Scientists have discovered something we have always suspected – reality TV lowers intelligence. We should be very concerned about the (**8**) ____________ of these shows. In the end, we could turn into the mindless zombies we watch on TV! — **WEAK**, **POPULAR**

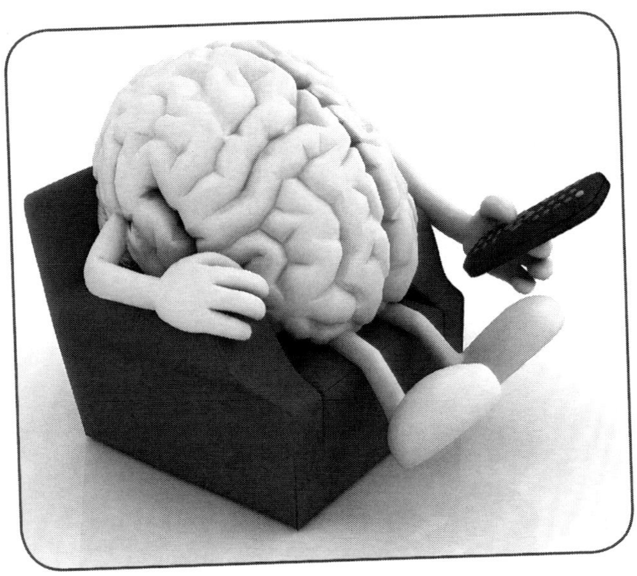

3 WRITING | A review

→ Student's Book, pages 34–35 → Writing reference, Student's Book, page 170

1 Complete the exam skill advice with the words in the box.

adjectives | example | explain | imagine | reasons

1 Good descriptions help your reader to ____________ exactly what you are talking about.
2 Use a range of ____________ to describe things. Don't just use simple adjectives.
3 Give ____________ and details. If you think something is amazing, clearly ____________ why and give an ____________ .

2 Read the review and write the paragraph (A–D) in the table.

	Purpose
Paragraph 1 ____	explain what you are reviewing and why
Paragraph 2 ____	give basic information about the series/film
Paragraph 3 ____	describe different aspects of the series/film and give your opinion
Paragraph 4 ____	give your recommendation

SMALLVILLE ★★★★☆ Today's best TV review

A The fact that Clark Kent isn't just an ordinary student makes the show more interesting. He has to deal with discovering his powers and keeping them secret as well as all the usual challenges of growing up. It explores themes such as friendship, loyalty and trust, and has thought-provoking dialogues. The action sequences are realistic and the special effects are convincing, which is not always true for older TV series.

B I'm a big fan of superheroes and I love high school dramas, so when I heard about *Smallville*, I decided to take a look at this series and find out if it was worth watching.

C I would definitely recommend this series to anyone who likes either superhero series or high school dramas. I'm sure you will enjoy it!

D *Smallville* tells the story of a teenage Clark Kent before he became Superman. The title comes from the town where he grew up. There were 10 seasons of the show before it stopped in 2011, and I like the first four seasons the most because they focus on Clark Kent's high school years.

3 Unscramble these words to make descriptive adjectives from the review.

1 raeltisic ____________
2 htugoht-voproinkg ____________
3 rindroya ____________
4 nocvgcinni ____________

4 Think of another TV series or a film and complete the paragraph plan.

	Purpose	Your notes
Paragraph 1	explain what you are reviewing and why	
Paragraph 2	give basic information about the series/film	
Paragraph 3	describe different aspects of the series/film and give your opinion	
Paragraph 4	give your recommendation	

PROGRESS CHECK

1 Write a modal verb from the box to complete each sentence.

can't | could | had to | is allowed to | must | ought to | shouldn't | will be able to

1 That ______________________ be my laptop computer; mine's definitely at home!
2 I wanted to leave a comment, so I ______________________ create a username and then write in the space.
3 You ______________________ be watching videos when you have a test to study for!
4 ______________________ you ______________________ leave soon? I'm in a hurry to get home.
5 It ______________________ be very boring making cooking videos; I'm sure I would hate it.
6 No-one in here ______________________ use my computer without my permission!
7 Of course I ______________________ make videos when I was 10! It really wasn't difficult.
8 I think you ______________________ get a better computer; this one doesn't edit very well.

2 Choose the correct words.

1 Editing videos is so tiring! Let's **do** / **make** / **take** a break and get some coffee.
2 All the most famous singers and bands perform on that **chat / music / talent** show every week.
3 Let's watch this video; the guy on it **says** / **tells** / **gives** some really good jokes!
4 The producers must spend a long time filming the animals for that **news / wildlife / weather** programme.
5 It will **do** / **have** / **make** us both good to spend less time online and more with our friends.
6 In this **game / reality / cookery** show people answer questions about their friends and try to win a holiday to the USA.
7 What a stupid video that was! No-one except Chris **saw** / **felt** / **found** it funny.
8 The weather **show** / **forecast** / **programme** said it's going to rain all day tomorrow.
9 Would you like to **make** / **have** / **take** part in a new music video that we are shooting?
10 There are too many **reality shows / talent shows / sitcoms** on TV. I'm not interested in what ordinary people do all day.
11 Stop **having** / **taking** / **making** fun of your cousin online; it's very mean!
12 There was a fascinating **sitcom / soap opera / documentary** about the history of the English language on TV last night.
13 After we have uploaded the video, let's **find** / **have** / **take** some friends round to watch it.
14 Julia got the recipe for her spaghetti Bolognaise from watching that Italian **weather / cookery / music** show.
15 Do you always **check** / **find** / **go** online and watch videos in the evening?
16 Some of the best actors on TV work in **soap operas / game shows / reality shows** these days.

Cumulative progress 1 2 3 4 5 6 7 8 9 10 11 12

3 Choose the correct word or phrase for each gap.

Tech-lovers unite!

Welcome to San Diego Comic-Con International. It's the place where comic lovers (**1**) ___________ come together to celebrate their passion. It (**2**) ___________ to be a comic book convention, but now includes video games, movies and TV shows. The organisers have succeeded (**3**) ___________ the event extremely (**4**) ___________ and now more than 100,000 fans attend each year. Many dress up like their favourite comic and video game characters, but you (**5**) ___________ dress up in order to attend. Fans can meet the creators of their favourite heroes or the actors from TV shows, many of whom say it's great to (**6**) ___________ part in the convention. The thing that makes the event special is its (**7**) ___________. Who knows … if you check it out, you (**8**) ___________ find that you enjoy it too.

	A	B	C	D
1	do	can	could	would
2	was	had	seemed	used
3	make	making	in making	to make
4	unpopular	popularly	popular	popularity
5	shouldn't	can't	mustn't	don't have to
6	take	have	make	find
7	origin	originality	original	originally
8	shall	ought	might	should

4 Big city life

READING | Open questions

→Student's Book, pages 36–37

1 Skim the text opposite for one minute then cover it and choose T (True) or F (False) for sentences 1–4.

1 The text is about things to do in different cities. **T / F**
2 The text is probably from a magazine. **T / F**
3 The text seems to be aimed at teenagers. **T / F**
4 The text doesn't give any specific information such as prices or exact locations. **T / F**

2 Read the text again. Write a short answer for each question. Use a maximum of four words.

1 Where can you 'drive' a public service vehicle?

____

2 Which place is in a famous area for putting on plays?

____

3 If you want to learn about the origins of a food, what should you go on?

____

4 How long have people been going to the fun parks?

____

5 Where's a good place to buy things to help you remember your holiday?

____

6 Which place is actually below street level?

____

7 Where would you have to get through crowds to buy something for a cheap price?

____

3 Complete the sentences with highlighted words from the article.

1 I'm not sure where my glasses are, I'll have to ____________ for them. I hope I find them!
2 I love French ____________ . It's my favourite style of cooking.
3 Do you want to take a photo? Where shall I ____________ ?
4 That shop always has all the latest fashions; it has the ____________ clothes in town.
5 I'm ____________ for a part in a film. I hope I get it – maybe I'll be a famous star!
6 I get ____________ phone calls after 6 pm. I phone my friends in the evenings, so my bill isn't expensive.
7 This is an ____________ painting. It's real; it isn't a copy or a fake.
8 Ted is extremely determined to get what he wants; he's so ____________ . He can be really unpleasant when he's trying to get you to do something.

I ♥ NY NEW YORK, NEW YORK!

Here are our tips for your visit to the Big Apple, as New York is known. Enjoy!

Eating

New York has been a centre of world cuisine for years. So make the most of it!

- The Food Court at Grand Central Station has everything from sushi to Indian to Caribbean food – check out their amazing Jamaican food patties for a new taste sensation. Prices are very reasonable.
- If you must have pizza, then go on the NYC pizza tour. As well as trying pizza at various restaurants, you'll learn about the history of pizza. Mmm!

Shopping

- St Mark's Place in the East Village near New York University is one of the trendiest – and cheapest – shopping areas. It's great for T-shirts, jewellery and cool young designer clothes.
- For the finest fashions at cut-rate prices, try Century 21 department store in Lower Manhattan. You have to hunt for the best bargains and it's usually packed, but it's worth it.
- If you're feeling adventurous, you could try the shops in Canal Street for souvenirs. Be warned, the salespeople can be rather pushy.

Museums

Museums can be fun!

- The New York Transit Museum, devoted to the history of public transport, is big and impressive. The museum, opened in 1976, is actually in a tunnel of an old subway (underground) station.
- You can enjoy exhibitions of vintage transport, tours and workshops – and you can pretend to drive a bus. At less than $10, the ticket charge is money well spent.
- At Madame Tussauds you can pose with wax models of your favourite stars, including Johnny Depp and Angelina Jolie. Or how about auditioning on an authentic *American Idol* set (and buying a DVD of your performance!)?

Chilling out

- People have been going to the beaches and fun parks in Coney Island to relax since the 1920s – you should too! A four-hour unlimited-rides ticket costs $35.
- Times Square is famous for its bright lights, shopping and theatres – now you can star in a 15-second video shown on the 7.6 m high screen there!

4 GRAMMAR 1 | Tense review: present perfect simple and continuous

→ Student's Book, page 38 → Grammar reference, Unit 4, Student's Book, page 151

1 Choose the correct words.

1 I wonder where the boys are. I've **waited** / **been waiting** for them outside the cinema for ages!
2 We've already **looked** / **been looking** at three flats this week, but we can't decide which one we want.
3 Mum's tired because she's **gardened** / **been gardening** all morning and it's hot outside.
4 For me, Rome is the most beautiful city in Europe; that's why I've **visited** / **been visiting** it so many times.
5 Kally hasn't **found** / **been finding** the right building for her new flower shop yet.
6 The Smiths have **built** / **been building** their new house for three months now.
7 Life in the countryside is boring and I've often **thought** / **been thinking** about moving to the city.
8 Joe has **learnt** / **been learning** Spanish since May because he wants to go to Madrid.

2 Complete the sentences using the correct form (present perfect simple or continuous) of the verbs in brackets.

1 I ______________ (**try**) to call Emily all morning, but I ______________ (**not have**) any luck. I wonder if she ______________ (**go**) to the library.
2 Sam ______________ (**go**) to a music school in the city centre for about a month. He ______________ (**have**) ten guitar lessons so far, but he ______________ (**not become**) a guitar legend yet!
3 Ellie ______________ (**not paint**) for long today, but she ______________ (**already, finish**) two rooms in her new flat. Unfortunately, she ______________ (**just, run out of**) paint!
4 ______________ (**you, see**) Ben today? It's his birthday and I ______________ (**not wish**) him a happy birthday yet. If you see him, can you tell him that I ______________ (**look**) for him?

3 Complete each sentence with the words in the box. Use each word only once.

already | ever | for | just | never | once | since | up | yet

1 Without a doubt, Santorini is the most beautiful island I have __________ been to.
2 I've only __________ realised that I left my guidebook on the bus!
3 We haven't been to the Natural History Museum __________ , but we really want to go.
4 Rosie will invite us to her new flat __________ she has moved in.
5 We're too late. The film has __________ started and they won't let us in.
6 I've __________ been to New York, but I'm looking forward to going soon.
7 __________ to now, only two families have shown any interest in buying our house.
8 We've been thinking about moving to the countryside __________ last summer.
9 Harry has been taking part in the city marathon __________ five years.

4 VOCABULARY | Topic vocabulary | Word patterns | Word formation

→ Student's Book, page 39 → Vocabulary reference, Student's Book, page 163

1 Choose the correct words.

1 **A:** Where does your Australian cousin live?
B: In the **city centres** / **suburbs** of Sydney.
2 **A:** Where do you live?
B: On the second floor of that **office block** / **block of flats**.
3 **A:** Are **services** / **attractions** like rubbish collection free where you live?
B: No! People have to pay for all those things.
4 **A:** Doesn't your sister work somewhere in this shopping **centre** / **store**?
B: Yes, she works in the shoe shop on the second floor.
5 **A:** Does your house have a garage?
B: No, but we always find a **car park** / **parking space** somewhere on our road.
6 **A:** Over a thousand people work in that **office block** / **block of flats**.
B: I'd like to get a job there when I leave school.
7 **A:** What can you see from your bedroom window?
B: I live opposite a huge **car park** / **parking space**, so not much!
8 **A:** Did you use the **subway** / **Tube** when you were in New York?
B: No, we either walked or went in one of the yellow taxis.
9 **A:** Are there any tourist **services** / **attractions** near where you live?
B: Yes, I live near the Eiffel Tower!

10 **A:** You can buy everything in that department **store** / **centre**.
B: I know! It's my favourite shop.

11 **A:** Let's walk to Buckingham palace.
B: No, I'd rather go on the **subway** / **Tube** as we're in London.

12 **A:** Do you know if there are any sports facilities in this area?
B: No, they're all in the **city centre** / **suburbs**, but we can easily go in by bus.

2 Complete each short text with two of the words or phrases in the box.

covered with | dispose | fed up | find a solution | have no intention | regardless

1 I know it can be very cold in Edinburgh, but I'm going ________________ of the weather. I've already booked my holiday and I ________________ of cancelling it.

2 Following the New Year's celebration in the city centre, the streets were ________________ rubbish. The city council had to send extra trucks to ________________ of it all.

3 The residents of the historic centre say they are ________________ with tourists making noise late at night, and they are asking the authorities to ________________ to this very annoying problem.

3 Complete the second sentence so that it has a similar meaning to the first sentence. Use a form of the word in bold in the first sentence.

1 I'm terribly sorry. I wasn't **aware** we were making so much noise.
I'm terribly sorry. I was ________________ we were making so much noise.

2 Since his fall, Charlie has not been **able** to walk.
Since his fall,Charlie has had a ________________ and cannot walk.

3 He **appeared** briefly and was never seen again.
He ________________ and was never seen again.

4 That chair doesn't look very **comfortable**.
That chair looks very ________________.

5 Margie isn't **able** to run fast.
Margie has an ________________ to run fast.

6 It's a definite **advantage** if you can drive.
It's a definite ________________ if you can't drive.

7 I couldn't **believe** what Freddy told me!
What Freddy told me was ________________!

8 Miles is only **able** to enter buildings with wheelchair access.
Without wheelchair access, Miles is ________________ to enter buildings.

9 Josh and Jo can't **agree** about where to live.
Josh and Jo ________________ about where to live.

10 The residents of the flats don't feel **secure**.
The residents of the flats feel ________________.

4 GRAMMAR 2 | Question review: question tags and question forms

→ Student's Book, page 41 → Grammar reference, Unit 4, Student's Book, page 151

1 Complete the sentences with the correct question tags.

1 Your friend Emma lives in a block of flats, ________________?

2 You've got a swimming pool in your back garden, ________________?

3 The view from the balcony isn't very good, ________________?

4 Nothing exciting ever happens in this town, ________________?

5 Let's rent a car and see the countryside, ________________?

6 Everybody loves a beach holiday, ________________?

7 Your brother will come to London with us, ________________?

8 Hardly anyone goes to the library these days, ________________?

2 Rewrite the questions correctly.

1 Which city Bruce liked the best on his trip?
____

2 Who did take these beautiful photos of Amsterdam?
____

3 Where in New York lives your cousins?
____

4 What happens when you lost your passport?
____

5 Why did you cancelled your trip to Barcelona?
____

6 How come did you decide to study in Tokyo?
____

7 What about walk to the museum?
____

8 How you know which bus to take?
____

4 LISTENING | Multiple choice (single extract)

→ Student's Book, page 40

1 Read the questions and responses and decide what each response means, a or b.

1 **A:** Did you find Melbourne boring?
B: On the contrary, it was quite lively with lots of interesting things to do.
a) No, I didn't. **b)** Yes, I did.

2 **A:** Would you say that large cities are dangerous?
B: Up to a point, but it's up to you to be careful.
a) Yes, definitely. **b)** Yes, partly.

3 **A:** Were the local people rude?
B: Absolutely not. They were extremely kind and helpful.
a) No way. **b)** I believe they were.

4 **A:** Is Cairo very noisy?
B: To a certain extent, but there are quiet places if you look for them.
a) No, not at all. **b)** No, not all of the city.

5 **A:** Do you think you will ever visit Buenos Aires again?
B: Definitely. There's a lot I didn't see the first time.
a) Yes, I intend to. **b)** Maybe.

6 **A:** Were the beaches clean?
B: Quite the opposite. I was very surprised.
a) Some were OK. **b)** No, they weren't.

7 **A:** Have you decided where you'll go?
B: Absolutely. I just need to book my ticket.
a) Yes, I have. **b)** I'm not sure yet.

8 **A:** Was the food in London OK?
B: Yes and no. I had a few nice meals.
a) Yes, it was very nice. **b)** Not all of it was good.

2 07 **Listen to a radio interview and choose the best answer (A, B or C).**

1 What does Matt say about the weather in Athens?
A He definitely wanted to experience it.
B It prevented him from doing a lot of things.
C He coped with it in the same way the Athenians do.

2 What surprised Matt about a museum he visited?
A the architectural style of the building
B some objects were not Greek
C a statue he only knew about from books

3 Why did Matt go to cafés so often?
A partly to get out of the sun
B to think about democracy
C to talk to Athenians

4 What does Matt believe led to democracy in Athens?
A the atmosphere when people had discussions
B it was a place of ideas and knowledge
C a combination of some important factors

5 What is Matt's view of Athens?
A It's too noisy for him.
B It's a city of contrasts.
C He can't understand the lifestyle.

4 SPEAKING | Discussion

→ Student's Book, page 42

1 Complete the phrases for agreeing and disagreeing with the words in the box. Then decide which phrases are for agreeing (A) and which are for disagreeing (D). Write A or D.

agree | a point | extent | forget | in that | opposite | point | true

1 That's ____________. ____
2 Let's not ____________ … ____
3 I think the ____________. ____
4 That's a good ____________. ____
5 I don't entirely ____________. ____
6 That's right up to ____________. ____
7 There's something ____________. ____
8 I agree to a certain ____________. ____

2 **Respond to the statements with a phrase for one of the following: agreeing and disagreeing, giving a reason, example or explanation.**

1 I think that in the future cities will become more polluted and overcrowded. ______________________

2 It's much nicer to live in a house than in a block of flats. ______________________

3 Life in a small town can be quite boring. ______________________

4 Public transport in my city is really good. ______________________

5 I think that having green areas like parks is really important for a city. ______________________

4 USE OF ENGLISH | Multiple-choice cloze

→Student's Book, page 43

1 **Choose the correct words.**

1 In Sydney you should **do** / **go** / **make** / **take** a tour of The Rocks. It's the historic area of the city **part** / **middle** / **centre** / **section**.

2 I really enjoyed going to the shopping **block** / **centre** / **space** with Nadia. There were so many department **shops** / **stores** / **places** / **spaces**.

3 There's good wheelchair **path** / **access** / **way** / **entry** to attractions, and plenty of **suburbs** / **services** / **blocks** / **subways** for disabled people.

4 Where do residents of **tower** / **tall** / **high** / **raised** blocks hang out their washing or **remove** / **throw** / **rid** / **dispose** of their rubbish?

5 Let's just take the train. I have no **aim** / **plan** / **intention** / **wish** of paying for a parking **area** / **space** / **zone** / **room** in the city.

2 **Choose the correct word for each gap.**

WEIRD AND WONDERFUL FACTS ABOUT FAMOUS SIGHTS!

Did you know that …?

The (**1**) ___________-famous Colosseum in Rome was originally called the Flavian Amphitheatre. It was named after the family of emperors who (**2**) ___________ sure that the people of Rome had a (**3**) ___________ building where they could enjoy free entertainment. Many people assume it got its name from its size since 'colossal' means huge. That's true (**4**) ___________ to a point, but the name came from a huge statue of Nero that stood nearby.

The Romans needed a strong material to build huge structures. They (**5**) ___________ a solution when they invented concrete. It was a (**6**) ___________ invention when the Colosseum was built and the Romans weren't sure how long it would last.

The outside of the Colosseum was (**7**) ___________ with an attractive stone. Over the centuries it was removed and used for other buildings that still exist. (**8**) ___________ of the fact that two-thirds of the Colosseum has gone, it remains one of the most impressive buildings of the ancient world.

1 **a)** earth **b)** all **c)** world **d)** well

2 **a)** made **b)** felt **c)** were **d)** knew

3 **a)** social **b)** people's **c)** society **d)** public

4 **a)** in **b)** up **c)** on **d)** around

5 **a)** found **b)** did **c)** made **d)** brought

6 **a)** fresh **b)** sudden **c)** recent **d)** late

7 **a)** formed **b)** made **c)** filled **d)** covered

8 **a)** However **b)** Regardless **c)** Although **d)** Despite

4 WRITING | An essay

→ Student's Book, pages 44–45 → Writing reference, Student's Book, page 174

1 Choose the correct words to complete the exam skill advice.

1 Examples make it **harder** / **easier** for the reader to understand your argument. They make your ideas **more convincing** / **vaguer**.

2 You **have to** / **don't have to** give different types of examples, e.g. advantages, problems, etc. You **can't** / **can** give examples from your own experience.

2 Read the essay below and decide if the sentences are T (True) or F (False).

1 The writer believes public spaces are not a good idea. **T / F**

2 The writer doesn't give any examples of advantages. **T / F**

3 The writer uses at least three different expressions for giving examples. **T / F**

Should cities have public spaces?

In cities, space for accommodation and businesses is very important. However, I believe that using land in cities for public spaces, such as big squares and parks, is essential for city living.

Public spaces have many advantages. Firstly, you can hold events like concerts, art exhibitions and sports competitions. These events create a feeling of community. Secondly, they are an ideal free place for exercising. For instance, parks are great for walking, cycling and ball games. As a result, people stay healthier. Finally, they make neighbourhoods more attractive and allow people to come into contact with nature.

On the other hand, creating and maintaining public spaces is expensive. In addition, they must be well designed and safe if you want people to use them. What's more, in city centres many businesses argue that they need the space to develop and consequently improve the local economy.

In conclusion, I believe the advantages of public spaces far outweigh the disadvantages. In my opinion, they are one of the key ingredients of a good quality of life for people there.

3 Write one word in each gap to complete the phrases for giving examples.

1 Some cities, such ___________ Madrid, have serious traffic problems.

2 Public transport that does not use the road, for ___________ the underground, is a great idea.

3 There are cities where people are encouraged to use bikes instead of cars. Amsterdam is an ___________ of this.

4 Other cities, ___________ Tokyo in Japan and Seoul in South Korea, have excellent transport systems.

4 Read the exam task. Decide if each point is about an advantage (A) or disadvantage (D). Then complete the sentences with your own examples.

What are the advantages and disadvantages of living in a capital city?

1 ☐ There are lots of things to do and places to see, such as ___________________________ .

2 ☐ There is usually a lot more pollution. For instance, as ___________________________ .

3 ☐ There is often more crime, for example ___________________________ .

4 ☐ Different types of public transport, like ___________________________ , are usually very good.

5 ☐ Traffic jams can be a serious problem. For example, ___________________________ .

6 ☐ Capital cities are often more expensive places to live. ___________________________ is an example of this.

PROGRESS CHECK

1 Complete the words in the sentences. The first letter is there to help you.

1 London, which is the c _ _ _ _ _ _ _ city of England, was named 'Londinium' by the Romans in the 1st century AD.

2 Believe me, I have no i _ _ _ _ _ _ _ _ _ of moving to the city; I prefer the peace and quiet of the countryside.

3 Because I live in a b _ _ _ _ of f _ _ _ _ , I can usually hear the TV from the flat above.

4 If you come by car when you visit, remember there are no p _ _ _ _ _ _ _ s _ _ _ _ _ _ in our street.

5 I can't understand why you're so interested in creating a v _ _ _ _ _ _ _ city. It's just a game, and a total waste of time.

6 Don't worry! I'm sure we can find a s _ _ _ _ _ _ _ to the problem together.

7 Which of the main tourist a _ _ _ _ _ _ _ _ _ _ _ _ do you plan to visit when you're in London?

8 Living in the s _ _ _ _ _ _ _ isn't so bad, but I'd rather be in the city centre, where there's lots to see and do.

2 Choose the correct word or phrase for each gap.

1 I've read two guidebooks __________ , but I still need more information.
a) yet **b)** since **c)** so far

2 Read out the phone number of the hotel to me, __________ you?
a) may **b)** would **c)** should

3 I'll phone you __________ I've checked in to my hotel.
a) as soon as **b)** already **c)** just

4 Who __________ the city 'New Amsterdam'?
a) did name **b)** named **c)** was named

5 I __________ all day; that's why I'm tired.
a) have been sightseeing **b)** sightseeing **c)** have to sightsee

6 __________ go to Barcelona again this year, shall we?
a) Shall **b)** Could we **c)** Let's

7 How come __________ visited London?
a) have you not **b)** you didn't **c)** you've never

8 I'm so terribly sorry. I'm late, __________ ?
a) aren't I **b)** don't I **c)** am I

Cumulative progress 1 2 3 4 5 6 7 8 9 10 11 12

3 Write one word in each gap.

Is Venice vanishing?

Every year, little by little, Venice **(1)** __________ sinking into the water. This unique city in the north of Italy has **(2)** __________ fighting against the water for hundreds of years; in fact, **(3)** __________ the 5th century when the city was founded. Will it lose the battle? Or **(4)** __________ scientists find a solution to stop the floods?

About four or five times a year, floods occur along Venice's canals. Because of this, residents often **(5)** __________ to walk on wooden boards to stay above the water. Many no longer use the basements in their houses. Although they are **(6)** __________ to the situation, the flooding is getting worse every year.

But what exactly is causing the problem? The ground on which Venice **(7)** __________ built is sinking, while at the same time the Adriatic Sea is rising because of climate change. These two factors working together are threatening the future of the city.

Let's hope that science will rescue Venice, **(8)** __________ we?

5 The weekend starts here!

READING | Multiple choice

→Student's Book, pages 48–49

1 Find and underline the phrases in italics in the article opposite. Then write the words in italics next to the things they refer to (a–g).

1 … our lives are very much determined by *this period*.
2 But why do we measure what we do in our lives in *this way* …
3 *They* are all based on natural phenomena:
4 Each of *these* lasts approximately seven days, so *that* could be the explanation.
5 *This* may have been for religious reasons because …
6 In Rome, however, *it* was named after the planet Mars, …

a) dividing it up into weeks ______
b) the phases of the moon ______
c) Tuesday ______
d) introducing a seven-day week ______
e) a week / seven days ______
f) days, months and years ______
g) the fact the phases of the moon last about seven days ______

2 Read the article again. For questions 1–5, choose the answer (A, B, C or D) which you think fits best according to the text.

1 According to the writer,
  A it is clear why we use a period of seven days to talk about time.
  B the other time periods we use are all explained by the sun.
  C a week is a natural phenomenon, like days, months and years.
  D people are used to organising their lives by weeks.

2 The Babylonians
  A knew that each phase of the moon lasted seven days.
  B definitely followed a calendar based on the moon.
  C were among the first people to have a seven-day week.
  D did not know about the existence of the month.

3 The seven heavenly bodies were
  A the reason the Babylonians celebrated rituals every seven days.
  B definitely the reason the Chinese started using the seven-day week.
  C known in China and Japan before they were known in Babylonia.
  D of no significance at all in the Babylonian civilisation.

4 The seven-day week
  A was always used by the Ancient Romans.
  B was used in the Roman Empire after 321 AD.
  C took centuries to spread to the rest of the world.
  D was commonly used before Constantine became emperor.

5 What does 'It's a similar story' in line 53 refer to?
  A All the days of the week are named after planets.
  B The names for the days of the week all come from the Romans.
  C The Norse god Thor named the days of the week.
  D Most names for weekdays derive from the names of planets or gods.

3 Find words or phrases in the article which match these definitions or explanations.

1 controlled or influenced (paragraph 1) ____________
2 things that can be seen to happen or exist (paragraph 2) ____________
3 indicates, shows (paragraph 2) ____________
4 relating to the moon (paragraph 3) ____________
5 periods of time in the development of something (paragraph 3) ____________
6 formal ceremonies (paragraph 3) ____________
7 something that is done a lot and considered normal (paragraph 4) ____________
8 ancient stories (paragraph 5) ____________

Wonderful Week

'What are you doing next week?' is a common question. We're used to our calendars being divided into weeks, and our lives are very much determined by this period. But why do we measure what we do in our lives in this way and where do the names of the week come from?

The origin of days, months and years is easily explained. They are all based on natural phenomena: the rising and setting of the sun for days, the cycle of the moon explains the concept of a month, and of course the time the Earth takes to travel round the sun is what marks a year. Could there be a similar explanation for the week?

History tells us that the Babylonians were one of the earliest civilisations to adopt a seven-day week. It is claimed that they followed a lunar calendar based on a period of what we know as a month and further divided this month according to the four phases of the moon: the new moon, half-moon, full moon and waning half-moon. Each of these lasts approximately seven days, so that could be the explanation. However, another theory points to the importance of the seven known heavenly bodies (the sun, moon, Mars, Mercury, Jupiter, Venus and Saturn) in Babylonian culture. As a result, they celebrated their rituals every seventh day and integrated this cycle into their calendar. Ancient China and Japan may have adopted the seven-day week for similar reasons.

The Ancient Romans initially used an eight-day week as part of their calendar. However, Constantine, the first Christian Roman emperor, introduced a seven-day week in 321 AD. This may have been for religious reasons because Christianity and some other religions believe the world was created in a week. Whatever the case, it became common practice in the Roman Empire and spread across the world.

The names of the days of the week are easier to explain. In most cultures, they come from names of gods or planets. For example, the English word Tuesday comes from the name of the Norse god Tiw (Tiw's day became Tuesday). In Rome, however, it was named after the planet Mars, so we have *martes* in Spanish, and *mardi* in French.
It's a similar story for other days. Thursday *line 53*
also gets its name from Norse mythology, namely Thor, the god of thunder, famous these days due to a whole series of Hollywood movies.

One thing is for sure, modern life depends on the existence of the week and having days with names makes it much easier to tell everyone what we are going to do and when!

5 GRAMMAR 1 | The future (1): *will, be going to,* present simple and continuous

→ Student's Book, page 50 → Grammar reference, Unit 5, Student's Book, page 152

1 Look at the phrases in bold and choose the correct use for each one, a or b.

1 That's a lot of equipment you have there. **I'll help you carry it** to the car.
a) a request
b) an instant decision

2 Don't worry about falling. The ropes are strong and **I'll be here** if anything happens.
a) a timetabled future event
b) a promise

3 Be careful, Ben! **You're going to drop the telescope** if you carry it like that!
a) a prediction based on evidence
b) an intention

4 Look! Here's a notice about some new art classes. **Shall we enquire** about them?
a) a suggestion
b) an arrangement

5 'Do you think they'll have fun DJing?' 'They **should**. It's a great thing to do!'
a) an instant decision
b) a prediction of probability

6 **I'm going to take up yoga** because I find it quite fascinating.
a) an intention
b) a prediction based on evidence

7 A new gym has opened in town. **Will you join with me**?
a) an offer
b) a request

8 I'm sure that **scuba diving in the Great Barrier Reef will be very exciting**!
a) a prediction
b) an instant decision

9 **We're going to pick up our new caravan** on Friday. I can't wait!
a) an arrangement
b) a suggestion

10 Hurry up, Eva! **The film starts in five minutes**!
a) a refusal
b) a timetabled future event

11 You're new here, aren't you? **I'll show you round** if you like.
a) a promise
b) an offer

12 You have to go to karate classes with me. **I won't go without you**!
a) a request
b) a refusal

2 Complete the sentences with the words and phrases in the box. Use each one only once.

are getting | are going to get | get | will get

1 I'm sure you ______________ an invitation to Cate's wedding. Don't worry – it's probably in the post.
2 You ______________ a new boat on Saturday. Really? That's fantastic news!
3 You ______________ a shock when you see Jimmy next week. He's lost 20 kilos since joining the gym.
4 Harry and Tod will join us as soon as they ______________ back from football practice today.

3 Choose the correct word or phrase.

1 **A:** Jess and Tim are excited. They **could have** / **are having** their first tennis lesson today.
B: Yes, I know. Let's ask them about it afterwards, **shall** / **will** we?

2 **A:** I **buy** / **'m going to buy** the concert tickets next Monday.
B: Get them now. I'm pretty sure there **aren't** / **won't be** any left by Monday.

3 **A:** Unless it **rains** / **will rain**, we'll go sailing this weekend.
B: I hope it doesn't, but I'm afraid it **might** / **shall**.

4 **A:** Oh, no! Look out! The football **is hitting** / **is going to hit** that spectator!
B: I think that player **catches** / **will catch** it first … yes! Well done!

5 **A:** How **are we making** / **are we going to make** a video without equipment?
B: I know! We **are using** / **'ll use** our phones!

6 **A:** I don't have enough money, so I **'m not going** / **don't go** to the cinema.
B: Oh, dear! Well, don't worry. I **will lend** / **'m lending** you some.

5 VOCABULARY | Word formation | Phrasal verbs | Topic vocabulary

→Student's Book, page 51 →Vocabulary reference, Student's Book, page 164

1 Complete the sentences with the correct form of the words in brackets.

1 When it's time to __________ our house, Dad always does it. He enjoys it because it's creative and it __________ his imagination. (**decor, stimulus**)

2 The thought of exercising doesn't __________ me at all. In fact, I __________ exercise with torture! (**motive, equal**)

3 I was __________ to get fit, so I took up jogging. On the first day, I fell and hurt my knee. I was __________ that it wasn't serious. (**despair, fortune**)

4 Once you __________ your account, you can play different brain games and __________ how good you are with words and numbers. (**active, value**)

5 Helen is a __________ person, who is always thinking of others. She's also very __________ towards her friends and gives them hugs. (**consider, affection**)

2 Write one or two words in each gap to complete the phrasal verbs.

1 It really gets me __________ when my team loses!

2 We need to sort __________ our plans for the weekend.

3 Dad, what do you remember most when you look __________ your university years?

4 The film was so boring that the person in front dropped __________ !

5 My parents don't stand __________ impolite behaviour.

6 I don't feel __________ going out this evening, to be honest.

7 You're always putting people __________ . Why are you so mean?

8 Did your mum let you __________ when you broke her phone?

3 Write the hobbies and interests next to the correct phrases.

blogging | board games | DJing | martial arts | mountain biking | online gaming
painting | photography | programming | scuba diving | social networking | yoga

1 ... then roll the dice and move on two squares. __________

2 ... and remember to breathe deeply and relax as you stretch. __________

3 ... I always try and use a variety of colours and brushes. __________

4 ... it's important to write about things you are interested in. __________

5 ... you can play with people from all over the world. __________

6 ... she posts updates and uploads videos about ten times every day. __________

7 ... it can be a lot easier to go downhill but it can also be more dangerous. __________

8 ... most people download the music but I don't. I prefer to mix records. __________

9 ... and the tropical fish I saw were amazing. __________

10 ... I think this is my favourite. I took it on safari in Africa last summer. __________

11 ... it's an ancient Japanese sport that can help you defend yourself. __________

12 ... it's a really useful skill that will help you get a job in I.T. __________

5 GRAMMAR 2 | Comparatives and superlatives

→Student's Book, page 53 →Grammar reference, Unit 5, Student's Book, page 153

1 Choose the correct words.

1 I like going to the gym, but it isn't as **fun as** / **much fun as** playing football with my friends.

2 Scuba diving is probably **more exciting** / **the most exciting** activity I have ever done.

3 I can swim **more** / **much** faster than my dad.

4 Martial arts are **more dangerous** / **the most dangerous** than you realise.

5 Yoga can be difficult, but the more you practise, **more relaxed** / **the more relaxed** you become. With time, it becomes **easier** / **easier than** to do.

2 Complete the dialogue with the correct comparative or superlative form of the words in brackets.

A: Was your trip to Italy (**1**) __________ (**good**) as you were hoping?

B: Actually, it was (**2**) __________ (**good**) I expected. I had a fantastic time!

A: Was it crowded?

B: Oh, yes! (**3**) __________ (**popular**) sights were all full. But if I went out (**4**) __________ (**early**) in the day, there were (**5**) __________ (**few**) people. Italy is (**6**) __________ (**beautiful**) country I've ever visited.

5 LISTENING | Multiple choice (extracts)

→ Student's Book, page 52

1 **Complete the sentences with the words in the box. Use the words in italics to help you.**

extent | eye | point | principle | wavelength

1 I've stopped going to the cookery class. I just *didn't see eye to* ____________ *with* the instructor. ____
2 Mum thinks I'll enjoy archery. I *agree to a certain* ____________, but if I find it boring, I'll stop. ____
3 My friend and I share lots of common interests and we *are really on the same* ____________. ____
4 I *agree in* ____________ with the idea that everyone should have a hobby they love, but I realise that lots of people are too busy to take up a hobby these days. ____
5 I know you think scrapbooking is boring, and that*'s true up to a* ____________, but it can be interesting, too. ____

2 **Look at the phrases in italics in Exercise 1 again. Do they show agreement (A), partial agreement (P) or disagreement (D)? Write A, P or D.**

3 08 **You will hear people talking in five different situations. For each question, choose the best answer (A, B or C).**

1 You hear two people talking about scrapbooking.
What do they disagree about?
A how the hobby got its reputation
B how people become interested in it
C how interesting the hobby is

2 You hear a man talking about his hobby.
What does he think about some famous stars?
A He can understand why some of them want privacy.
B He doesn't think they are genuine.
C He finds them annoying.

3 You hear two friends discussing an activity.
What are they going to do together?
A appear on television
B train to become chefs
C attend a cooking class

4 You hear two friends talking about what to do.
What do they agree about?
A They will meet their friends at the shopping centre.
B They want something interesting to do.
C They want to see the same film.

5 You hear a woman talking to some students.
What is the woman's advice?
A make time for a hobby
B try to attend university
C stop physical activities while you study

5 SPEAKING | Interview

→ Student's Book, page 54

1 **Choose the correct words.**

1 My ambition is to **go** / **go to** university in the United States.
2 It's important to **get** / **take** a good job after you graduate.
3 I'm not interested in **becoming** / **having** rich and famous.
4 I would like to **become** / **get** married at the age of 30.
5 Big families are great! I want to **have** / **make** six children!
6 I would really love to **travel** / **travel to** the world.

2 **Complete the words in the dialogues. The first letter is there to help you.**

1 **A:** What are you doing this w _ _ _ _ _ _ _ ? Anything exciting?
B: Well, I don't have any s _ _ _ _ _ _ _ _ plans, but I'm h _ _ _ _ _ _ to get out and enjoy the fresh air.

2 **A:** Have you thought about what you'd like to do in the f _ _ _ _ _ _ ?
B: I'm not s _ _ _ yet. I like the idea of helping people, so maybe I'll become a teacher.

3 **A:** Are you p _ _ _ _ _ _ _ _ to study medicine at university?
B: Yes, I am. It's my a _ _ _ _ _ _ _ _ to become a doctor one d _ _ .

4 **A:** Are you looking f _ _ _ _ _ _ _ to getting a job and becoming independent?
B: Definitely. At some p _ _ _ _ , I'd like to have a career and my own home.

3 **Write your own answers to the questions in Exercise 2.**

1 ______________________________
2 ______________________________
3 ______________________________
4 ______________________________

5 USE OF ENGLISH | Open cloze

→ Student's Book, page 55

1 **Choose the correct words.**

1 I'll be waiting for you **out of** / **outside** the theatre, **at** / **on** exactly seven o'clock.
2 I heard you recently took **off** / **up** stamp collecting. I'm also interested **for** / **in** stamps.
3 Are you involved **in** / **to** any afternoon activities **after** / **before** school, such as art or sport?
4 There's nothing interesting to watch **at** / **on** TV tonight. Shall we go **away** / **out** instead?
5 **In** / **With** your free time, what sort of sports do you like to take part **in** / **on**?
6 When I need a break, I chill **about** / **out** by painting or listening **at** / **to** music.
7 The best thing about the weekend is that I can stay **at** / **in** bed regardless **of** / **on** the time.
8 David took a week **off** / **from** work and went sailing **from** / **with** friends.
9 The bookshop is **between** / **in** the post office and the bank, just **across** / **around** the road from the bus stop.
10 It always gets me **down** / **off** when the holidays end and I have to return **at** / **to** school.

2 **Write one word in each gap.**

I don't really get **(1)** __________ to much when I have free time, but I often watch TV. And there is one TV show that I never miss. It's *Law & Order*. I'm sure you've heard **(2)** __________ it. It's a police drama series that takes place in New York. It's been **(3)** __________ TV for a really long time; in fact, ever **(4)** __________ I can remember. I'm fairly certain it's one of the longest running shows on TV right now.

Every Monday **(5)** __________ 8.30 pm exactly, I get comfortable in front **(6)** __________ the TV and enjoy another episode. No-one in my house is allowed to disturb me **(7)** __________ it's finished. Then they can watch whatever they like. Sometimes **(8)** __________ the weekend, if I'm lucky, there's a *Law & Order* marathon. Episode after episode … that's a great weekend!

5 WRITING | An article

→ Student's Book, pages 56–57 → Writing reference, Student's Book, page 169

1 **Choose the correct words to complete the exam skill advice.**

1 When you give an opinion, it's important to provide your **beliefs / reasons**.

2 You can use phrases like *The reason* ***for / of*** *this is* … and *This is* ***right / because*** …

2 **Read the article. Underline three examples of giving reasons and circle six examples of contractions.**

Getting active in your free time

Do you spend most of your free time sitting at home? Many young people do – and when they go out, it's to sit in a café or cinema! That's because they're not used to doing anything active. If this sounds familiar, then here are some reasons for getting active.

First of all, because you are so busy at school, you feel tired and it's tempting to spend your free time watching TV or on the computer. Don't! Instead, take up a sport. It gets you out of the house and you'll get physically fit and feel more energetic.

Secondly, you will learn new skills. You will learn the physical skills you need for the sport, but you will benefit in other areas too! The reason for this is that when you learn something new, you stimulate the brain. This helps your memory and can make you more creative and better able to respond to challenges.

Finally, sport is also good for your social life because whatever kind of sport you do, you will meet new people.

Enjoy being active!

3 **Read the exam task. Then complete the sentences with the words in the box.**

You see this notice on an English-language website for teenagers.

Making the most of your free time
We all know teens don't have much free time these days. But what advice would you give young people to get the most from their free time? The best articles will appear on our website!

Write your **article**.

about | because (× 2) | reason | suggest | thing

1 Many teens don't have much free time. The ___________ for this is that they are busy with school.

2 Make a note of everything you do every day for a week. This will help you ___________ you will see exactly where you are wasting time.

3 Cutting down on the time you spend using electronic gadgets will help. That's ___________ most young people spend far too long every day using them. How ___________ only looking at your texts twice a day?

4 I ___________ you choose one activity you want to do and make a timetable for your day.

5 Another ___________ you could try is to set aside time for doing activities, and don't use this for homework.

4 **Write a first paragraph for the exam task in Exercise 3.**

____

____

____

____

____

PROGRESS CHECK

1 Choose the correct words.

1 My granny is very loving and **affection** / **affectionate** whenever we visit her.
2 Bad weather at the weekend really **gets me down** / **puts me down** because I can't go anywhere.
3 Am I the only one who feels such **despair** / **desperate** when my team loses?
4 They're both fun, but I prefer **board games** / **online gaming** because you don't have to stare at a screen all the time.
5 Jane took me to a boring lecture about Shakespeare and I **got off** / **dropped off** in the middle of it!
6 Don't you **equal** / **equate** the school holidays with summer and travel? I know I do!
7 Sabrina has always kept a diary so it was easy for her to take up **programming** / **blogging**.
8 This is a complicated problem and I don't know how to **sort it out** / **look back on it** . Do you have any ideas?
9 I had the good **fortune** / **fortunate** to meet Roger Federer and that's when I became interested in tennis.
10 I'm not going to Joe's party tonight because I just don't **stand for** / **feel up to** it, I'm afraid.
11 Brain games are great because they **stimulus** / **stimulate** the mind and sort of train it to become better.
12 The coach will **value** / **evaluate** our progress before deciding who will be chosen to play in Friday's match.

2 Choose the best answer, a, b or c.

1 I can't do this exercise. __________ you help me with it, please?
a) Do **b)** Shall **c)** Will
2 'Do you think I'll win the race?' 'You __________ do. You're the best swimmer!'
a) should **b)** might **c)** may
3 How can we find a guitarist for our band? I know! __________ an ad online.
a) I'm putting **b)** I'll put **c)** I put
4 The moment that we __________ the door, shout 'Surprise!' as loudly as you can.
a) open **b)** will open **c)** are going to open
5 __________ I help you to clean up after your party?
a) Do **b)** Might **c)** Shall
6 Don't you think football is __________ harder to play than table tennis?
a) more **b)** much **c)** most
7 __________ we leave, the less traffic there'll be on the road.
a) The sooner **b)** Sooner than **c)** The soonest
8 Ed will be a great basketball player. How much __________ do you think he'll grow?
a) tall **b)** taller **c)** tallest
9 In my opinion, the theatre isn't __________ the cinema.
a) exciting as **b)** more exciting **c)** as exciting as
10 I have to say, that was the __________ performance I have ever seen.
a) worst **b)** worse **c)** worse than

Cumulative progress 1 2 3 4 5 6 7 8 9 10 11 12

3 Choose the correct word for each gap.

ABOUT ME | CONTACT | BLOG | PHOTO ALBUMS ▾

DO SUNDAY BLUES EXIST?

Posted at 9:00 on 4th January

Have you ever heard of the Sunday blues? I (**1**) __________ about it recently in an online article. It's a feeling of anxiety or sadness (**2**) __________ by thinking too negatively about the week ahead that really (**3**) __________ people down. When you think about it, it's a logical thing. I mean, who looks (**4**) __________ to going back to school or work after a weekend?

One thing is for certain, I usually don't (**5**) __________ up to much on Sundays. I tend to stay in bed late and even when I get up, it takes me a long time to actually (**6**) __________ going. I usually stay at home (**7**) __________ of the weather and have a lazy day.

However, my friend Emily believes the answer is exercise. She believes that (**8**) __________ a Sunday doing nothing actually makes the Sunday blues worse, and that exercise releases chemicals in the brain that fight 'the blues'. She's convinced me to join her for a bike ride next Sunday to see if she is right. I'll keep you posted …

1 **A** studied **B** found **C** read **D** researched
2 **A** happened **B** made **C** provoked **D** caused
3 **A** lets **B** makes **C** gets **D** puts
4 **A** ahead **B** onwards **C** forward **D** after
5 **A** feel **B** look **C** take **D** stand
6 **A** get **B** start **C** begin **D** become
7 **A** despite **B** in spite **C** however **D** regardless
8 **A** waiting **B** passing **C** spending **D** doing

6 Good food, good mood

READING | Multiple choice

→Student's Book, pages 58–59

1 Find these sentences in the article opposite. Choose the best word or phrase to complete each description.

1 *Of course, some of the things we hear do have an element of truth in them, even when they're factually incorrect.*

The use of 'even when' suggests a contrast, so the word 'element' here probably means **a small amount** / **a lot** / **nothing**.

2 *It contains flavonoids which can help prevent some cancers and heart disease, as well as counteract high blood pressure.*

The first part of the sentence describes some positive health effects of dark chocolate. The second part of the sentence begins with 'as well as', and high blood pressure is a health problem, so the word 'counteract' here probably means **increase** / **reduce** / **worsen**.

3 *If you eat carrots, you won't have eyes like Superman. However, it'll help you avoid tripping over things in the dark!*

The word 'However' indicates contrast, and 'avoid' means 'prevent from happening'. So 'tripping over' probably means **seeing** / **finding** / **falling over**.

4 *Have you ever heard that and fretted that the gum you once swallowed was still inside you?*

The word 'that' refers to the idea in the previous sentence (*gum stays inside you for years*), which is a scary idea, so the word 'fretted' probably means **worried** / **laughed** / **been happy**.

If gum is inside you, then the word 'swallowed' probably means **ate** / **vomited**.

2 Choose the correct word. If you aren't sure, find the highlighted words in the article and deduce the meaning.

1 euphoric	extremely **happy** / **sad**
2 arose	**ended** / **started**
3 pinpoint	find the **exact** / **approximate** position of something
4 enemy	a country that is **friendly** / **at war** with another country
5 dissolved	when a solid substance becomes **mixed with** / **separated from** a liquid
6 eliminated from	**put outside** / **keep inside** something

3 Read the article again. For questions 1–5, choose the answer (A, B, C or D) which you think fits best according to the text.

1 Some food myths

A are definitely the result of true facts.

B are based on something that is partly true.

C are hard to understand.

D are unrelated to a healthy diet.

2 Why does chocolate make us feel good?

A Because it contains chemicals that make us feel happy such as phenylethylamine.

B Because when we have insufficient 'happy' chemicals, it helps us feel better.

C Because it has a positive effect on our health, so we feel better.

D Because eating it has an effect on the part of the brain that responds to feeling good.

3 Eating carrots

A will hugely improve your night vision.

B has no effect on your eyes at all.

C is good for your eyes because of the Vitamin A.

D helped pilots see better in wartime.

4 Which is true about drinking water?

A You should drink eight glasses of water a day if you want to stay healthy.

B It's important to drink water, but not necessarily eight glasses.

C You should drink lots of water because there isn't any in fruit and vegetables.

D You should only ever drink water when you feel thirsty.

5 The expression 'wreak havoc' in the section about gum means it would

A have a very bad effect on the body.

B make operations more difficult for surgeons.

C make it harder for food to be dissolved.

D prevent the digestion of other food.

www.check...

Nutrition Myths

Everyone wants to have a healthy diet, but these days we get so much information about food and good food habits that it's hard to know what is and isn't true! Of course, some of the things we hear do have an element of truth in them, even when they're factually incorrect.

Eating chocolate has the same effect as falling in love

If we feel happy, the brain releases phenylethylamine and serotonin into the nervous system. They're the chemicals that make us feel happy or even euphoric, just like we feel when we fall in love. Chocolate also contains these chemicals, so many people have claimed it has the same effect on the human body. However, the quantities of these chemicals in chocolate are insufficient to affect us. The latest research shows that the effects of eating chocolate are in fact psychological, rather than physiological – the smell, texture and taste of chocolate make eating it a pleasant experience, which stimulates the emotional 'feel-good' centres of the brain. Chocolate tastes good, so we feel content. And chocolate fans will be even happier to know that dark chocolate has health benefits. It contains flavonoids which can help prevent some cancers and heart disease, as well as counteract high blood pressure.

Carrots allow you to see in the dark

Sorry, but eating carrots doesn't give you the superhuman power of night vision! This myth arose during World War II, when the authorities claimed that British pilots could see in the dark because they ate so many carrots. They did this to hide the fact that they had developed a new form of radar that could pinpoint the position of enemy planes. However, it is true that carrots contain Vitamin A, which helps your eyes work well in low light conditions. If you eat carrots, you won't have eyes like Superman. However, it'll help you avoid tripping over things in the dark!

You need to drink eight glasses of water a day

This is one myth that just won't go away – and it has no basis in fact! Of course, you need to stay hydrated, but you don't need eight glasses of water to do that. When this recommendation was made, doctors hadn't taken into account that we get water from fruit and vegetables, as well as from other drinks like tea and coffee. If you have a healthy diet and drink water when you feel thirsty, you'll be fine!

Gum stays in your stomach for seven years

'If you swallow gum, it'll stay in your stomach for years!' Have you ever heard that and fretted that the gum you once swallowed was still inside you? Well, stop worrying! Of course, if gum stayed in your body, it would wreak havoc on it, but luckily it's just a myth. Everything we eat is dissolved and eliminated from the body within a day, including gum. Although surgeons have occasionally seen a piece of gum in the digestive system, it's never more than a few days old.

So now you know!

6 GRAMMAR 1 | Conditionals (1): zero, first and second conditionals

→ Student's Book, page 60 → Grammar reference, Unit 6, Student's Book, page 153

1 Match the conditional sentences to the situations they describe.

1 If she doesn't do any training, she won't be ready for the marathon! ____
2 If I stay out in the sun for too long, I always get sunburnt. ____
3 If you didn't eat so much junk food, you'd be a lot healthier. ____
4 If you heat water to 100 °C, it boils. ____
5 If the fish is not fresh, don't buy it! ____

a) general truth
b) scientific fact
c) real or likely situation
d) commands, instructions and advice
e) hypothetical, impossible or unlikely situation

2 Choose the correct words.

1 If you **drank** / **drink** eight glasses of water a day, you'd feel better.
2 Take a banana with you in case you **get** / **got** hungry later.
3 If Reggie gets a migraine, he always **stays** / **will stay** at home.
4 Unless the doctor is busy, she **would** / **will** see you at two o'clock.
5 Is it true that if you **ate** / **eat** an apple a day, you won't get sick?
6 If you **have** / **had** a cup of warm milk before bed, you should sleep better.
7 If I were really fit, I **can** / **could** run a marathon.
8 Eating junk food is OK as long as you **won't** / **don't** do it regularly.

3 Complete the second sentence with one word so that it means the same as the first sentence.

1 I want to go out today but I can't because I'm not well enough.
I __________ go out today if I were well enough.
2 Put on some sun cream because you might burn.
Put on some sun cream in __________ you burn.
3 Taking this medicine would make the pain go away.
If you __________ this medicine, the pain would go away.
4 If you don't eat well, you won't be strong and healthy.
__________ you eat well, you won't be strong and healthy.
5 I won't go to the dentist if you don't come with me.
I'll go to the dentist as __________ as you come with me.
6 I'll cook chicken unless he's vegetarian.
If he is __________ vegetarian, I'll cook chicken.

6 VOCABULARY | Word patterns | Word formation | Topic vocabulary

→ Student's Book, page 61 → Vocabulary reference, Student's Book, page 164

1 Complete the dialogues with the prepositions in the box. Use the words in italics to help you. You will use some words more than once.

against | for | of | on | to

1 **A:** Would you like one of these peanut cookies? I made them myself.
B: I'd love to, but I can't. I'm *allergic* __________ peanuts.

2 **A:** I feel terrible. I can't seem to *get rid* __________ this cold.
B: Have you tried hot tea with lemon and honey?

3 **A:** My dentist doesn't *approve* __________ me eating sweets.
B: Well, he's absolutely right!

4 **A:** You drink a lot of coffee. It can't be good for you.
B: It isn't, but I really can't stop drinking it. I'm *addicted* __________ it.

5 **A:** This new research is *based* __________ an earlier study.
B: I see. Are the results the same?

6 **A:** What does your cousin do?
B: He's a scientist. He's trying to find a *cure* __________ cancer.

7 **A:** This old wives' tale *dates back* __________ the 12th century.
B: Amazing! And people still believe it!

8 **A:** I would strongly *advise* __________ going to the beach without sun cream.
B: Don't worry. I've got some in my bag.

2 **Complete the text with the correct form of the words in brackets.**

The Mediterranean: more than just sea and sunshine

Have you heard of the Mediterranean diet? It's not a diet to lose weight, but a way of life that helps people to live (**1**) ___________ (**relative**) longer, healthier lives. The great thing about it is that it is (**2**) ___________ (**surprise**) easy to follow. (**3**) ___________ (**basic**), it involves being physically active, getting up (**4**) ___________ (**early**), (**5**) ___________ (**regular**) enjoying meals with others and eating fresh food (**6**) ___________ (**day**).

Much of the food in the Mediterranean diet is (**7**) ___________ (**remarkable**) effective in preventing health problems. The diet is based on fresh fruit and vegetables, grains, beans, nuts, herbs, fish and seafood, cheese and yoghurt. Processed foods and too much red meat are avoided. (**8**) ___________ (**tradition**), red meat was only eaten on special occasions, and not as (**9**) ___________ (**frequent**) as it is now.

So give the diet a try and (**10**) ___________ (**hope**) it will help you achieve a happy, healthy lifestyle.

3 **Complete the words in the sentences. The first letter is there to help you.**

1 You often get a s _ _ _ t _ _ _ _ _ and a high t _ _ _ _ _ _ _ _ _ _ when you have the flu.
2 Winston got a nasty b _ _ _ _ _ on his leg and also s _ _ _ _ _ _ _ his ankle when he fell over playing football.
3 Millie was shaking and had a nasty f _ _ _ _ for five days. It was probably a v _ _ _ _.
4 Lots of people catch a c _ _ _ in the winter but it usually isn't serious.
5 It's important to be careful in the kitchen. You might c _ _ your finger on a sharp knife or b _ _ _ your hand on the hot oven.
6 Students with a food a _ _ _ _ _ _ _ should tell the kitchen staff before they have lunch.
7 After sitting on a bus for five hours Harry had a painful c _ _ _ _ in his left leg, but it soon went once he started walking again.

6 GRAMMAR 2 | Relative clauses

→Student's Book, page 63 →Grammar reference, Unit 6, Student's Book, page 154

1 **Choose the correct words.**

1 The food we ordered, **that** / **which** was expensive, was terrible!
2 July is **when** / **where** many people in Europe go on holiday.
3 The beach **which** / **where** we went to was amazing.
4 I don't know the reason **why** / **that** she won't take her medicine.
5 Jon is the person **who** / **whose** you should ask about dieting.
6 The stadium **that** / **where** they played the match was quite small.
7 Leo, **whose** / **whom** sister is a vegetarian, loves eating red meat!
8 The café in **where** / **which** Oscar works only serves healthy food.

2 **Complete the second sentence so that it has a similar meaning to the first sentence, using relative pronouns.**

1 The local chemist recommended this cough syrup.
The person ___________ recommended this cough syrup was the local chemist.
2 Eggs are a source of protein and easy to cook.
Eggs, ___________ are a source of protein, are easy to cook.
3 My friend has great teeth and his brother is a dentist.
My friend, ___________ brother is a dentist, has great teeth!
4 My grandmother stayed in a hospital that was new.
The hospital in ___________ my grandmother stayed was new.
5 We are doing research with a Japanese scientist.
The scientist with ___________ we are doing research is Japanese.
6 The doctor didn't explain the reason the blood test was necessary.
The doctor didn't explain ___________ the blood test was necessary.
7 The doctor prescribed me painkillers but they weren't very effective.
The painkillers ___________ the doctor prescribed weren't very effective.
8 I visited an optician last week but he wasn't very good.
The optician ___________ I visited last week wasn't very good.

6 LISTENING | Multiple choice (extracts)

→ Student's Book, page 62

1 09 **Listen to the speakers and choose the word that describes their attitude.**

1 Speaker 1 is **happy** / **confused**.
2 Speaker 2 is **grateful** / **worried**.
3 Speaker 3 is **surprised** / **sad**.
4 Speaker 4 is **scared** / **angry**.

2 10 **Listen to the extract. Then choose the correct words.**

1 The woman is presenting **her own** / **a common** attitude towards home remedies.
2 When the woman says 'I am a fool and I don't care who knows it,' she **really believes** / **doesn't actually believe** she is a fool.
3 Overall, her attitude is **in favour of** / **against** home remedies.

3 11 **You will hear people talking in five different situations. For each question, choose the best answer (A, B or C).**

1 What is the woman's attitude towards home remedies?
A She finds them ridiculous.
B She thinks that there are good reasons to use them.
C She thinks she is foolish to use them.

2 How does the girl feel about modern medicine?
A She never takes it.
B It helped her cough.
C She would rather avoid it.

3 What is true about the woman and her doctor?
A They have a friendly relationship.
B They like to talk about the weather.
C They disagree about her treatment.

4 Why is the woman annoyed with the man?
A He isn't really sick.
B He looked at the wrong website.
C He has done something he shouldn't have.

5 What is the boy sorry about?
A that he is very sick
B that he has let his coach down
C that someone will replace him

6 SPEAKING | Photo task

→ Student's Book, page 64

1 **Choose the correct words.**

1 I'd **not prefer** / **prefer not** to go cycling.
2 I prefer outdoor activities **over** / **for** indoor ones.
3 I would **rather** / **prefer** swim than jog.
4 My preference would be **with** / **for** walking.
5 I'd never go **for** / **to** long distance running.

2 **Complete the sentences with the words and phrases in the box.**

because | because of | due to the fact | so | the reason for me

1 ______________________ not choosing jogging is because I find it boring.
2 I wouldn't choose swimming ______________________ I'm not good at it.
3 I'd never choose walking ______________________ that it rains a lot here.
4 I love team sports ______________________ I'd definitely choose football.
5 I would probably choose hiking ______________________ my interest in nature.

3 **Look at the photos in the exam task below. Make notes to complete the table.**
Student A: Compare the two photographs and say how you think the people in the pictures feel.
Student B: Which of the two ways of keeping fit would you prefer? Why?

	Activity A	Activity B
Positive aspects		
Negative aspects		
How do the people in the photo feel?		
Which activity would you prefer?		
Why?		

6 USE OF ENGLISH | Word formation

→ Student's Book, page 65

1 **Decide if the word in bold is an adjective (ADJ) or an adverb (ADV).**

1 Martin enjoys running and is training **hard** for a marathon. ________
2 I've got a headache, a sore throat and a fever. I feel **awful**! ________
3 If you start exercising, your health will **gradually** improve. ________
4 Jess is really tired, so she's going to have an **early** night. ________
5 Darren is a **fast** swimmer and he might win the race. ________
6 The cost of the gym membership is **unlikely** to change. ________
7 I'm tired today because I didn't sleep **well** last night. ________
8 Don't worry, you'll be alright – a broken arm is **easily** fixed. ________
9 I agreed to drink some carrot juice, but it tasted **disgusting**. ________
10 Grandad was **anxious** about the results of his blood tests. ________

2 **Write a form of the word in capitals in each gap.**

FUEL FOR LIFE

We all know the importance of eating a healthy diet – and that's fairly **(1)** ____________ to do when we live at home with our family. Not **(2)** ____________ , however, a lot of young people struggle when they leave home for college or work and have to shop and cook for themselves **(3)** ____________ . It's very tempting to eat convenience foods and fast food, but **(4)** ____________ that won't do you any good. Food is fuel and we shouldn't underestimate the **(5)** ____________ importance of putting the correct fuel into our bodies. Our bones and muscles depend on it for growth and **(6)** ____________ . Food affects how fit we feel, how much energy we have and, **(7)** ____________ , how well our brains perform.

There are plenty of old wives' tales about food, but you could do worse than eating an apple a day. In fact, eating fruit and vegetables **(8)** ____________ is a good place to start if you want to change your eating habits and fuel your body for life!

EASE
SURPRISE
REGULAR
BASIC
ORDINARY
STRONG
REMARK
FREE

→ Student's Book, pages 66–67 → Writing reference, Student's Book, page 169

1 **Read the exam task and the article. Then tick the things the writer has done.**

You see this notice in an English-language magazine for teenagers:

> **Articles wanted**
> We're looking for articles about tips for getting through your exams, including ideas on how to stay healthy.

Write your **article**.

1 ☐ addressed a question directly to the reader to engage them
2 ☐ used a friendly style that's not too formal, and included the reader (e.g. using *you*, *your* and contractions)
3 ☐ divided the information into five clear paragraphs
4 ☐ included some expressions with exclamation marks (!) for emphasis
5 ☐ concluded the article in a suitable way

BEATING EXAM STRESS

How often have you heard someone say, 'I am so stressed about these exams'? Exams are never easy but there are a number of things you can do to make sure your health does not suffer as a result.

One of the best ways of overcoming exam stress and anxiety is to be well prepared. Make a realistic revision schedule, with regular breaks every 30 minutes. You'll learn more if you take breaks, because your brain will be fresh. Eating well is also really important. Don't have too much sugar or caffeine and avoid fatty foods like burgers and chips. Instead, eat plenty of fresh fruit and vegetables, cereals and oily fish such as salmon – they're good for your brain! Also, remember to drink plenty of water – if you don't, you get dehydrated and that can give you a headache. Finally, rest and relaxation are also very important. You shouldn't study all day without stopping. Make sure you get at least eight hours' sleep every night – you'll feel better for it!

So, the next time you have exams, follow these tips. Good luck!

2 **Read the middle section of the article in Exercise 1 again. Mark the places where you should divide it into three paragraphs.**

3 **Look at the exam task below and the paragraph plan. Match two ideas from the list (a–f) to paragraphs 2, 3 and 4.**

You see this notice in an English-language magazine for teenagers:

> **Articles wanted**
> We're looking for articles on the importance of getting a good night's sleep and how to go about it.

Write your **article**.

Paragraph 1	introduction – engage the reader and introduce the topic
Paragraph 2	talk about the importance of having a good bedtime routine ____ ____
Paragraph 3	talk about making your bedroom a good place to sleep ____ ____
Paragraph 4	finish by saying ways to relax ____ ____
Paragraph 5	conclusion

a) Go to sleep at the same time every night.
b) Write a 'to do' list for tomorrow, so you can clear your mind and stop worrying.
c) Don't watch TV in bed – in fact keep technology out of your room.
d) Doing the same thing (e.g. having a shower, having a warm drink) every evening tells your brain it is time to get ready for sleep.
e) Read a book; this can help to distract the mind.
f) Make sure the room is not too hot.

4 **Write an engaging title and introduction for the article in Exercise 3.**

____

____

____

PROGRESS CHECK

1 Choose the correct words.

A: You look (1) **unhappiness** / **unhappy**. What's wrong?

B: I've got a nasty cold and I can't seem to get rid (2) **of** / **on** it. I've tried everything.

A: Unfortunately, there's no cure (3) **to** / **for** the common cold.

B: Is that (4) **true** / **truly**?

A: Yes, it is. The only thing you can do now is to make yourself (5) **comfortably** / **comfortable** in bed and make sure you drink plenty of hot tea with lemon. (6) **Hopeful** / **Hopefully**, you'll feel better in a few days.

B: Thanks for the advice, but I need to be (7) **best** / **well** by tonight. I've been invited to Matt's party and I don't want to miss it.

A: I would advise (8) **about** / **against** going out. Based (9) **in** / **on** what the doctor said to me when I had a cold, it can make you worse if you go out.

B: What if I only go to the party for a little while? Just an hour or two? Would you approve (10) **for** / **of** that?

A: Well, no, I wouldn't, but it's your decision. If you're worse tomorrow, it'll be your own fault!

2 Choose the best word to complete each sentence.

1 If you ___________ to the chemist's, get me some aspirin.
a) went **b)** are going **c)** would go

2 I'll be really angry if Anna ___________ all the apples!
a) will eat **b)** might eat **c)** has eaten

3 I wouldn't eat so many sweets if I ___________ you.
a) am **b)** were **c)** will be

4 If you climb trees, you ___________ break your arm!
a) could **b)** shall **c)** should

5 ___________ you drink milk, your bones will be weak.
a) As long as **b)** In case **c)** Unless

6 If you weren't well, I ___________ you, of course.
a) would help **b)** helped **c)** will help

7 The clinic in ___________ Isla works is very modern.
a) where **b)** which **c)** that

8 The nurse with ___________ I spoke was very helpful.
a) whom **b)** that **c)** who

9 Swimming, ___________ is great exercise, is also fun.
a) that **b)** whose **c)** which

10 That time ___________ I cut my hand, I was chopping vegetables.
a) where **b)** when **c)** why

11 The doctor ___________ checked my ears and throat.
a) I saw **b)** that saw **c)** which he I saw

12 That woman ___________ daughter lives near me is a chemist.
a) who **b)** that **c)** whose

Cumulative progress 1 2 3 4 5 6 7 8 9 10 11 12

3 Choose the correct word for each gap.

FOOD ALLERGIES

When it comes to your diet, milk, eggs, nuts, fish and seafood can all play an important role in maintaining good health. The protein and other essential nutrients aren't a cure (1) ___________ illnesses, but they can help you stay well, or recover faster when you're ill. Surely, it can only (2) ___________ you good to eat them regularly. Sadly, that's not true for everyone. One in 50 people suffer from food allergies. Based (3) ___________ scientific research, we now know that 90% of those sufferers are allergic (4) ___________ milk, eggs, nuts, fish and seafood.

Allergy sufferers who eat these foods can (5) ___________ up with nasty symptoms. Common allergic reactions to these foods include skin rashes, in which the body (or a part of it) becomes covered (6) ___________ spots, but in extreme cases, eating these foods can cause the body to go into shock. It only takes one thousandth of a single peanut in food to cause serious problems in such cases, and can even cause death.

Unfortunately, food allergy sufferers cannot simply (7) ___________ rid of their allergies by taking medicine, so they must (8) ___________ about their daily lives being extremely careful about what they eat. Fortunately, these days a lot of food packaging warns buyers which potential allergy-causing ingredients they contain.

1 **A** to **B** from **C** in **D** for
2 **A** have **B** do **C** make **D** seem
3 **A** on **B** by **C** in **D** with
4 **A** at **B** from **C** to **D** for
5 **A** come **B** end **C** show **D** look
6 **A** from **B** at **C** on **D** with
7 **A** have **B** send **C** get **D** go
8 **A** go **B** be **C** walk **D** try

7 Best friends forever

READING | Gapped text

→Student's Book, pages 70–71

1 Decide how each phrase is used. Write H for saying when things happen, Cl for giving clarification, R/C for giving a result/consequence and CO for introducing a contrast.

After that,	H	As a result,	____	On the other hand,	____
Apart from that,	____	Before long,	____	That is to say,	____
As a consequence,	____	In other words,	____	To begin with,	____

2 Read the sentences and choose the correct explanation.

1 *As a result, he started spending time with other friends and they drifted apart.*
This sentence **explains the consequence of** / **clarifies** something in the previous sentence.

2 *Before long, everyone knew.*
'Before long' tells us **when** / **why** something happened, and 'everyone knew' refers to something **becoming public** / **staying private**.

3 *In other words, friendship is a two-way relationship.*
This sentence is intended to **give a result of** / **clarify** something in the previous sentence.

4 *Of course, you can say it kindly.*
'Of course' introduces an idea which follows **logically** / **illogically** from the previous sentence.

3 Read the text opposite. Choose which sentence A–G fits each gap 1–6. There is one extra sentence you do not need.

A As a result, he started spending time with other friends and they drifted apart.
B This is hard, especially because you might be worrying about how they will react.
C Before long, everyone knew.
D In other words, friendship is a two-way relationship.
E Apart from that, it helps build trust.
F Of course, you can say it kindly.
G In addition to that, it's important not to judge them for what they have done or said.

4 Find these words in the text and write a definition for each one.

1 depend on (paragraph 2) ______________________
2 ruined (paragraph 2) ______________________
3 mess up (paragraph 3) ______________________
4 forgave (paragraph 3) ______________________
5 behaviour (paragraph 5) ______________________
6 feedback (paragraph 5) ______________________
7 at risk (paragraph 6) ______________________
8 betrayed (paragraph 6) ______________________

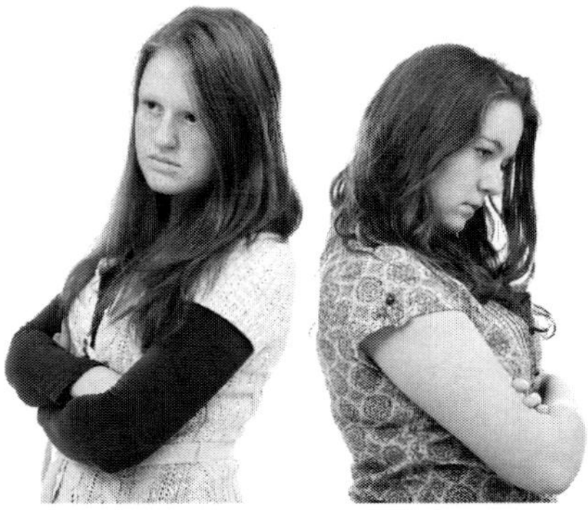

HOW TO BE A GOOD FRIEND

'If you want to have a good friend, then be a good friend', so the saying goes. 1 ______ If we want to have good friends, then we have to behave towards our friends as we want them to behave towards us.

One of the important ingredients of a friendship is trust. If you say you will do something or be somewhere, then do it. Your friends have to know they can depend on you, no matter what. This is probably the number one reason friendships are ruined. As Joe, 17, says, 'I thought Matt and I would be best friends forever, but then he met Lucy. After they'd been going out for a few days, he started cancelling our plans to meet. He'd phone at the last minute and say something had come up.' Joe found out Matt was meeting Lucy instead. 2 ______

Of course, friends do mess up. In that case, the best thing to do is apologise – fast. Disappointing your friend, or saying something nasty hurts, but it's how you react after that is more important. 'I nearly lost my best friend Lexie,' explains Eva. 'She told me a secret, but I told another friend. 3 ______ Lexie was upset about that, but she was most upset that I'd broken my promise.' Eva admitted her mistake to Lexie and apologised for letting her down. In the end, Lexie forgave Eva and now their friendship is stronger than before.

Listen. If your friend has problems, then just listen. The best way is to try and understand the situation from your friend's point of view. 4 ______ You don't have to fix things and you shouldn't assume that your friend wants advice – they might just want to talk things over so they can decide what to do.

Tell the truth. Your friend wants your opinion – not what you *think* they want to hear. You might be the only person who will tell them an item of clothing doesn't suit them or that you don't like a certain sort of behaviour. 5 ______ Don't be cruel! Remember, friends rely on this kind of feedback to help them make good choices.

Lastly, be prepared to make hard decisions. That is to say, if you think your friend is making a serious mistake or is at risk, then you might need to get help from a parent, a teacher or someone in a position of responsibility. 6 ______ Will your friend feel betrayed by your actions? Remember, you're only doing this because you care and don't want them to get hurt.

7 GRAMMAR 1 | Tense review: past perfect simple and continuous

→Student's Book, page 72 →Grammar reference, Unit 7, Student's Book, page 155

1 Read each sentence and choose the statement that best explains what it means, a or b.

1 By the time I reached the phone, it had stopped ringing.

a) The phone rang and I went towards it.

b) I was going towards the phone when it rang.

2 Lily was angry because Adam had been lying to her for a long time.

a) Adam told more than one lie.

b) Adam told only one lie.

3 My friend had been talking for a few minutes when she started to cry.

a) She was crying while we were talking.

b) First she talked and then she cried.

4 The party guests weren't dancing because the DJ had left.

a) They stopped dancing and then the DJ left.

b) The DJ left, so the guests couldn't dance.

5 I had known Millie for a few weeks before we became Facebook friends.

a) I met Millie in real life first.

b) I met Millie on Facebook and then we became friends.

2 Choose the correct words.

1 It wasn't the first time Anna and Marie **had kept / had been keeping** us waiting.

2 By 10 o'clock when the tickets went on sale, we **had waited / had been waiting** for three hours.

3 I **hadn't heard / hadn't been hearing** about the get-together before Huw told me.

4 I was exhausted because I **had cleaned / had been cleaning** the house all day for the party.

5 **Had the film already started / Had the film already been starting** by the time you got there?

6 The argument was awful. It was the worst we **had ever had / had ever been having**!

7 I **hadn't eaten / hadn't been eating** sushi until my Japanese friend gave me some to try.

8 We **hadn't danced / hadn't been dancing** for long when the music suddenly stopped.

9 I didn't see Sam when I got home because he **had just left / had just been leaving**.

10 I **hadn't seen / hadn't been seeing** the Smiths because they were away on holiday.

3 Complete the dialogue with the correct tense (past perfect simple or continuous) of the verbs in the box.

be | forget | get to | have | look forward to | not take | spend | talk

Tess: Why are you so late? I **(1)** ______________________ that film all week, and I didn't want to miss it. Now it's too late.

Lena: I'm really sorry, Tess.

Tess: What happened?

Lena: Well, I **(2)** ______________________ the bus stop when I saw Nigel. You remember him, don't you? He **(3)** ______________________ my neighbour for years before his family moved to Australia. Well, he's back now to visit his grandparents. Naturally, we started chatting, you know. We **(4)** ______________________ a lot of time together when we were kids and we had plenty to talk about. By the time he left, we **(5)** ______________________ for over an hour!

Tess: Why didn't you call me?

Lena: I couldn't. I **(6)** ______________________ to take my phone with me when I left my house. I only realised I **(7)** ______________________ it when Nigel left and I wanted to call you.

Tess: I was really worried about you. I thought you **(8)** ______________________ an accident or something.

Lena: I'm really, really sorry. I promise it won't happen again!

7 VOCABULARY | Topic vocabulary | Word formation | Phrasal verbs

→ Student's Book, page 73 → Vocabulary reference, Student's Book, page 165

1 Choose the verb that best matches the statements.

1 'I think she's brilliant. She's patient, kind and always helps other people.' **rely on** / **admire**

2 'I need to tell you something really important but you mustn't tell anyone else.' **confide in** / **lose touch**

3 'It wasn't a nice thing to do and it upset me, but you're my best friend and that's more important.' **rely on** / **forgive**

4 'Have you heard about Carmen? She's got a new boyfriend and Petra says he's really good-looking.' **count on** / **gossip**

5 'Thank you so much for all the hard work you've done. I'm so grateful.' **appreciate** / **get on**

6 'I want to know that I'm here and I'm going to help you through this.' **share** / **support**

2 Complete the text with the correct form of the words in brackets.

The right friend

How many real friends have you got? How many offer (**1**) ___________ (**assist**) when you need it and give (**2**) ___________ (**encourage**) when you feel like giving up? Experts in human (**3**) ___________ (**develop**) recognise the importance of (**4**) ___________ (**relation**) you make in your teens. Although hanging out with popular kids seems cool, your (**5**) ___________ (**friend**) with them may not be meaningful. Being accepted by them is like (**6**) ___________ (**member**) of an exclusive club – but are they true friends? They're probably not interested in a (**7**) ___________ (**partner**) of equals; they might only need you to make them feel important. Your (**8**) ___________ (**prefer**) should be for someone who shares your interests and your outlook. That person could be a friend for life!

3 Complete the dialogues with the phrasal verbs in the box in the correct form.

drop in on | get along with | go round to | keep on | look up to | rip up | run after | take after

1 **A:** Who do you ____________________ ?
B: My mum – I've got her eyes!

2 **A:** It's so boring here! There's nothing to do!
B: Why don't we ____________________ Carl? He's home today and he's always good fun.

3 **A:** My ex-boyfriend has sent me a postcard!
B: I hope you __________ it __________ !

4 **A:** You ____________________ your grandfather, don't you?
B: Yes, I do. He's an amazing man!

5 **A:** I can't ____________________ Alice's new boyfriend.
B: Same here! I can't stand the guy.

6 **A:** Alfie ____________________ phoning me!
B: Yes, I've heard he's interested in you.

7 **A:** Look! That rabbit is ____________________ your friend. It's hilarious!
B: Quick! Film it and we'll put it on YouTube.

8 **A:** Are you doing anything later?
B: Yes, I'm ____________________ Dean's place.

7 GRAMMAR 2 | Connectors of contrast

→ Student's Book, page 75 → Grammar reference, Unit 7, Student's Book, page 155

1 Choose the correct words or phrases.

1 **Despite** / **Even though** we no longer attend the same school, we are still friends.

2 Sophia has managed to make some friends **in spite of** / **although** her shyness.

3 My sister prefers to be alone **despite** / **although** having a large number of friends.

4 I don't see Miles very often. He is, **however** / **even though**, still a close friend.

5 Nancy is a very trustworthy person **in spite of** / **although** she's still only a young teen.

6 **Even though** / **In spite of** the fact that we had an argument, we remain close friends.

7 **Although** / **Despite** having a very bad temper, Joel still manages to keep his friends.

2 Complete each sentence with one word.

1 I do like Matilda, in ___________ of the fact she can be cold sometimes.

2 Lucas used to be popular. ___________ , no-one seems to like him now.

3 ___________ though we fight a lot, my sister and I are actually very close.

4 I think it's great having lots of Facebook friends ___________ what some people believe.

5 ___________ Gran is in her 70s, she's still close to her best friend from childhood.

7 LISTENING | Multiple matching

→Student's Book, page 74

1 **Read what the speakers say and choose the statement (a or b) that best explains what they mean.**

1 'When Ed asked me out to the cinema in front of everyone, it was awkward and I couldn't say no.'
  a) I like Ed so I agreed to go out with him.
  b) It was an embarrassing moment for me.

2 'We can't possibly have an end-of-year celebration without inviting Bradley. He's the life and soul of the party!'
  a) Bradley is a good person to have in social situations.
  b) It isn't possible to invite Bradley to the event.

3 'John's sitting there all alone. Let's join him. He's new here and hasn't made any friends yet.'
  a) It's his preference to sit alone.
  b) We should be friendly towards him.

4 'What's up, Serena? Come on, you can tell me. You know what they say, *A problem shared is a problem halved*.'
  a) If you tell me about your problem, it will be easier to deal with.
  b) I can help you if we have a problem in common.

2 12 **You will hear five extracts about making friends. Choose from A–H what each speaker says about it. There are three extra letters you do not need.**

A I always seem to make the wrong friends.
B It was stressful for me to meet new people.
C I'm cautious when it comes to choosing friends.
D It makes me happy to help my friends.
E My friends and I have the same things in common.
F I feel bad about letting down a friend of mine.
G I make no effort to make new friends.
H The people I wanted to be friends with ignored me.

Speaker 1: ☐
Speaker 2: ☐
Speaker 3: ☐
Speaker 4: ☐
Speaker 5: ☐

7 SPEAKING | Collaborative task

→Student's Book, page 76

1 **Choose the correct word or phrase for each gap.**

A: OK, so let's discuss the characteristics that make a good friend. Would you like to go first?
B: Sure. Well, I think it's better if friends have similar tastes and interests.
A: **(1)** ___________ that people who don't have things in common can't be friends?
B: In a way, yes. I mean, if you don't like or do the same things, it's hard to spend time together.
A: Yes, I **(2)** ___________ your point. Personally, I think character is more important.
B: Could you explain **(3)** ___________ what you mean?
A: Well, for example, a good friend should always be honest with you.
B: Yes, I agree up to a point. Honesty is **(4)** ___________ important, but occasionally a friend may lie.
A: What do you **(5)** ___________ when you say that?
B: It's **(6)** ___________ that knowing the truth about something might hurt your feelings.
A: Could you give me an **(7)** ___________ ?
B: Well, you might be wearing something that doesn't look good, and you ask your friend what she thinks. It would be hurtful of her to say you look terrible!
A: Yes. You're right about that. But on the other hand, good friends shouldn't agree with you all the time.
B: **(8)** ___________ you mean they should have their own opinion? I completely agree!

1 **a)** Do you say **b)** Have you said **c)** Are you saying
2 **a)** realise **b)** see **c)** look
3 **a)** exactly **b)** truly **c)** totally
4 **a)** practically **b)** seriously **c)** extremely
5 **a)** suggest **b)** mean **c)** know
6 **a)** possible **b)** able **c)** maybe
7 **a)** instance **b)** opinion **c)** example
8 **a)** Do **b)** Are **c)** Shall

2 **Match to complete the phrases.**

1 Sorry, but I don't really see your ____
2 Do you mean that cool friends ____
3 Could you give me ____
4 Are you saying that you think ____
5 Could you explain exactly ____

a) friends should always agree?
b) what you mean about popularity?
c) point about common interests.
d) an example of that?
e) are better than honest friends?

7 USE OF ENGLISH | Sentence transformation

→ Student's Book, page 77

1 **Choose the correct tense for each gap.**

1 I was angry because I ______________________ with my friend all morning.
a) has argued **b)** has been arguing **c)** had been arguing
2 ______________________ those people before or was that the first time?
a) Had you met **b)** Have you met **c)** Do you meet
3 Rebecca and Ella ______________________ each other since childhood.
a) knew **b)** have known **c)** know
4 I ______________________ about their argument until you told me.
a) wasn't hearing **b)** haven't heard **c)** hadn't heard
5 We ______________________ for long when the phone line went dead.
a) haven't been talking **b)** hadn't been talking **c)** haven't talked
6 By midday, my lazy brother ______________________ for over 12 hours!
a) had been sleeping **b)** was sleeping **c)** has been sleeping

2 **Complete the second sentence so it has a similar meaning to the first. Do not change the word given. Use two to five words, including the word given.**

1 You have a lot of admiration for your friend's father, don't you? **LOOK**
You really ______________________ your friend's father, don't you?
2 Even though Jane can be cold at times, I still like her. **OF**
I still like Jane ______________________ occasional coldness.
3 Fred decided to leave the party before we arrived. **ALREADY**
By the time we arrived, Fred ______________________ the party.
4 Two years after he met her, he asked her to marry him. **HAD**
He ______________________ two years before he asked her to marry him.
5 Kate and her sister Leah have a very good relationship with each other. **ON**
Kate and her sister Leah ______________________ with each other.
6 Although they aren't very close, they do spend time together. **DESPITE**
They do spend time together, ______________________ very close.
7 I know James can always be relied upon to help me if I've got a problem. **COUNT**
I know I can always ______________________ to help me if I've got a problem.
8 Unfortunately, my best friend Mason and I haven't had any contact with each other since we left school. **TOUCH**
Unfortunately, my best friend Mason and I ______________________ when we left school.

7 WRITING | A story

→ Student's Book, pages 78–79 → Writing reference, Student's Book, page 173

1 Complete the exam skill advice with the words in the box.

continuous | descriptions | direct speech | variety

1 Past verb tenses are very important when you write stories or ________________ of events.
2 Use a ________________ of tenses, e.g. past simple, past perfect simple and ________________ .
3 ________________ gives you the chance to use other tenses.

2 Read the story and underline an example of these tenses:

1 present simple
2 past simple
3 past continuous
4 present perfect
5 past perfect
6 past perfect continuous

An unusual meeting

I hadn't been looking forward to it at all. We'd moved to a new town and I knew that in just a few days I'd be starting my new school. Everyone in my class had already been at the school for five years and they all had friends. Who was going to talk to me?

I went into town on my skateboard to get some shoes for school. Finally, I spotted a pair I liked. I was trying them on when I heard a voice.

'Have you got these in a size 10?' It was a boy about my age and he was holding the same shoes – not only that, but he was carrying a skateboard!

We both bought the shoes and as I was paying he said, 'Cool board!' We got talking about skateboarding and he told me about the best places to skate. It turned out that he lived near me and went to my new school. We met up and walked to school together on my first day and we've been best friends since then – all because of a pair of shoes!

3 Read the exam task below and then make notes to complete the plan.

You see this announcement on an English-language website:

Stories wanted!

We're looking for stories by talented writers. Your story must begin with this sentence:

I hadn't been looking forward to it at all.

Your story must include:

- an unexpected way of meeting a new friend
- an object that helps you meet

Write your **story**.

Part	Purpose	My notes
Title	briefly describe what the story is about – and make us want to read it	
Paragraph 1	copy the first sentence and set the scene (What hadn't you been looking forward to? Where? Why not?)	
Middle paragraphs	continue the story – say what happened and remember to include an object that helps you meet	
Final paragraph	finish the story – say what happened in the end and whether you are still friends	

PROGRESS CHECK

1 Complete the dialogues with the words in the box.

after (× 2) | in | on (× 2) | to | up (× 2) | with (× 2)

1 **A:** Why don't we go round ___________ Jake's place?
B: No, I'd rather not. I don't get along ___________ his brother.
2 **A:** You know you can always rely ___________ me to help.
B: Yes, I know that, and I really appreciate it. Thanks.
3 **A:** Have you heard from Simon recently?
B: No, I haven't. I lost touch ___________ him a few years ago.
4 **A:** I can see from this photo that you take ___________ your grandmother.
B: Yes, I do, and I look ___________ to her too.
5 **A:** Do you get ___________ well with your brother and sister?
B: Yes, I do. They're both really good friends.
6 **A:** I don't usually confide ___________ my colleagues at work, but I know I can trust you.
B: Yes, of course. Whatever you tell me is confidential.
7 **A:** Why were you running ___________ Ethan yesterday?
B: Because he ripped ___________ the card I gave him!

2 Choose the correct words or phrases.

1 I **had never been / had never been going** to a pyjama party before.
2 Bruce **had prepared / had been preparing** all day for the get-together.
3 I **hadn't heard / hadn't been hearing** the news about their engagement.
4 **Had you been dancing / Had you danced** for long when I arrived?
5 By the time Stanley got to the café, his friends **had already left / had already been leaving**.
6 **Even though / However** she's outgoing, she hasn't got a lot of friends.
7 **Despite / Although** the weather wasn't good, we didn't cancel the picnic.
8 Greg says some pretty stupid things **however / in spite of** his intelligence.
9 Character is important. **However / Although**, some people only care about looks.
10 **Despite / Even though** the fact that she is quiet, Carly can be very stubborn.

Cumulative progress 1 2 3 4 5 6 7 8 9 10 11 12

3 Write a form of the word in capitals in each gap.

ET the Extra-Terrestrial

Hollywood loves the topic of (**1**) ___________. Whether it's between teens or animals, films about friends have been (**2**) ___________ successful over the years. **FRIEND** **ORDINARY**

One of the most popular films of all time, *ET the Extra-Terrestrial,* is about the (**3**) ___________ between a quiet, lonely little boy and a loveable alien whose life he helps to save with the (**4**) ___________ of his family. The film looks at the (**5**) ___________ of the unique bond that forms between the boy, Elliot, and the alien, who he has named ET. **RELATION** **ASSIST** **DEVELOP**

Once Elliot gets over his shock at the (**6**) ___________ of aliens, he and ET become so close that they feel each other's emotions – a situation which produces some comic moments. **EXIST**

With his brother and sister helping him, shy little Elliot finds the courage to defy the authorities looking for ET, who is (**7**) ___________ to return to its home planet. **DESPAIR**

The actor playing Elliot gives a wonderful (**8**) ___________, as does ET! **PERFORM**

8 The only way is up

READING | Multiple matching

→Student's Book, pages 80–81

1 Find these sentences in the text opposite and read the sentences around them. For each one, choose the option that best describes what is implied.

1 *Then, knowing it was in some of the toughest, most remote mountainous terrain in the state, she decided to try to hike to safety.*
Rescuers **were likely to find / had very little chance of finding** the plane wreck.

2 *Although Autumn was traumatised by her experience, rescuers said she had been extremely lucky.*
Autumn has always been a lucky person. / People don't usually survive this kind of incident.

3 *It took him three and a half days, with no food and little water, to travel the eight kilometres.*
It was an extremely difficult journey. / He wasted a lot of time making the journey.

4 *After a long recovery, he got a prosthetic arm and still climbs today.*
His injuries **haven't changed his lifestyle / have seriously affected every aspect of his life**.

5 *When she heard a loud pop, she knew she was in trouble.*
The sound told her that **an avalanche had started / nothing important was happening**.

2 Read the text again. For each question, choose from the people A–D. The people may be chosen more than once.

Which person

1 was the most seriously injured? ☐
2 took immediate action to increase his/her chances of surviving? ☐
3 survived more than one accident in succession? ☐
4 first realised he/she was in danger because of a sound? ☐
5 had to walk for two days before being found by someone? ☐
6 has found that their personality changed as a result of surviving? ☐
7 fell over a steep drop on the mountain? ☐
8 had the quickest rescue? ☐

3 Find the words or phrases in the text and choose the correct meaning, a or b.

(paragraph A)

1 trail	**a)** a country path	**b)** a busy road
2 traumatised	**a)** severely shocked or frightened	**b)** unaffected

(paragraph B)

3 lower	**a)** use ropes to move something	**b)** move something down from a higher position
4 crevasse	**a)** a very deep crack in ice on a mountain	**b)** a type of cave
5 crawled	**a)** moved quickly	**b)** moved with difficulty on hands and knees

(paragraph C)

6 trapped	**a)** touched	**b)** caught
7 rappelling down	**a)** going down a steep slope using a rope	**b)** walking down a mountain

(paragraph D)

8 swept	**a)** carried quickly	**b)** moved slowly

www.theyactually...

SURVIVAL!

Mountains are wonderful places to visit, but they can be dangerous too. Today, we hear about four amazing survival stories.

A Autumn Veatch

In 2015, 16-year-old Autumn Veatch survived a plane crash in the mountains in Washington State, USA. Autumn waited a day in the hope that rescuers would find the plane. Then, knowing it was in some of the toughest, most remote mountainous terrain in the state, she decided to try to hike to safety. She eventually found and followed a trail for two days before reaching Highway 20. There, a motorist picked her up and drove her nearly 50 km to the nearest small town to alert the emergency services. Autumn was then taken to hospital for treatment for minor injuries. Although Autumn was traumatised by her experience, rescuers said she had been extremely lucky.

B Joe Simpson

In 1985, Joe Simpson and his climbing partner Simon Yates successfully reached the peak of Siula Grande in the Peruvian Andes, but on the way down Simpson broke his leg during a storm. Despite the dark and terrible conditions, Yates managed to lower Simpson most of the way down the mountain on a rope. Then disaster struck. Simpson went over a crevasse edge and Yates had to cut the rope to save himself. Simpson fell 45 metres, but did not die. He managed to climb out of the crevasse and then crawled over the snow and rocks to base camp. It took him three and a half days, with no food and little water, to travel the eight kilometres. He then faced a long operation in hospital. Three years later, he wrote a book about his experience called *Touching the Void*, which was made into a docudrama film in 2003.

C Aron Ralston

A keen climber, in 2003, Aron set off to climb and hike in the Canyonlands National Park, USA, without telling anyone his route. While he was climbing down a canyon, a huge boulder fell and trapped his right arm. Aron had very little food and water with him. After five days he managed to amputate his arm to free himself. Aron then had to make his way to safety, including rappelling down a 20-metre cliff. A rescue helicopter then took him to hospital, where he very nearly died. After a long recovery, he got a prosthetic arm and still climbs today. He says his accident made him a better, more humble person. His book, *Between a Rock and a Hard Place*, was made into the film *127 hours* in 2010.

D Emily Anderson

Emily Anderson was skiing with friends on Crystal Mountain near Seattle, USA, when she noticed the snow under her moving strangely. When she heard a loud *pop*, she knew she was in trouble. Seconds later, an avalanche swept her into a tree and she was buried under more than a metre of snow. The 20-year-old could only move her left hand slightly, but her quick-thinking in scooping the snow away from her face saved her. A friend had seen the accident and immediately alerted the ski patrol, who arrived within minutes. When they found Emily, she had been buried for 15 minutes but she was alive and unhurt. Her experience didn't stop her skiing – in fact, she wanted to get a job with the ski patrol!

GRAMMAR 1 | The passive

→ Student's Book, page 82 → Grammar reference, Unit 8, Student's Book, page 155

1 Complete the dialogues with the words in the box.

as | in | of | with

1 **A:** Did you know that Mount Everest is located in Nepal, Tibet and China?
B: I did. Did you know that it's known in Tibet ___________ Chomolungma?

2 **A:** These photos of the rock formations are incredible. Did you use a professional camera?
B: Actually, they were taken ___________ my mobile phone.

3 **A:** Are you sure the pegs to keep the tent in place are strong enough?
B: Absolutely. They're made ___________ metal and are very tough.

4 **A:** I've just read that parts of Everest are covered ___________ rubbish!
B: I've heard that too. Apparently, it's what climbers leave behind.

2 Complete each second sentence, using the passive, so that it means the same as the first sentence.

1 They're preparing the equipment now.
The equipment ______________________________.

2 They used to take the sheep to the mountains.
The sheep ______________________________.

3 No-one had stolen anything from the base camp.
Nothing ______________________________.

4 You shouldn't use these old ropes for climbing.
These ______________________________ for climbing.

5 A mule was carrying the supplies up the mountain.
The supplies ______________________________ a mule.

6 Have they found the climber yet?
Has ______________________________ yet?

7 I hated it when the leader told me what to do.
I hated ______________________________ the leader.

3 Put the verbs into the passive to complete the text.

Mighty Mount Olympus rises majestically from the surrounding Greek countryside. For most of the year, its peaks **(1)** ______________ (**cover**) in snow. It is a popular place for nature lovers and it **(2)** ______________ (**estimate**) that there are over 1,700 plant species there. It **(3)** ______________ (**climb**) by many over the years. Reaching the top-most peak, however, is something that **(4)** ______________ (**should not / attempt**) by inexperienced climbers. Despite its beauty, Olympus **(5)** ______________ (**know**) mainly as the home of the 12 Olympian gods of ancient Greece. It was from here that terrifying thunderbolts **(6)** ______________ (**throw**) by Zeus. Olympus is where the gods gathered when punishments **(7)** ______________ (**have to / hand out**) to the humans below. Understandably, the ancient Greeks feared the mountain and the idea that it **(8)** ______________ (**can / conquer**) by humans was not one they considered.

8

VOCABULARY | Topic vocabulary | Word formation | Word patterns

→ Student's Book, page 83 → Vocabulary reference, Student's Book, page 165

1 Complete the words in the sentences. The first letter is there to help you.

1 In the summer, there isn't much water in the s _ _ _ _ _ that runs past our house.
2 All along the south c _ _ _ _ there are lots of c _ _ _ _ _ that rise over 100 metres above the sea.
3 In winter lots of people ski down the s _ _ _ _ _ on this m _ _ _ _ _ _ _ _ r _ _ _ _ .
4 Walkers can follow the p _ _ _ up the mountain. The views from the s _ _ _ _ _ are spectacular.
5 It's very dangerous to swim near the w _ _ _ _ _ _ _ _ _ in the river.
6 Between the two mountains there is a beautiful v _ _ _ _ _ with a river flowing through it.
7 You can sometimes see steam and smoke coming out of the top of the v _ _ _ _ _ _ _ .

2 **Complete the dialogues with the noun form of the words given.**

1 conclude | vary

A: There is considerable ___________ in the ability of the climbers.

B: I came to the same ___________ myself; it's not an ideal situation.

2 arrive | depart

A: Our ___________ in Kathmandu was delayed by bad weather.

B: Oh, dear. Was your ___________ from Nepal similarly affected?

3 behave | describe

A: The ___________ of the local guides is said to be quite extraordinary.

B: Yes, there's an amusing ___________ of it in the explorer's autobiography.

4 choose | solve

A: Did they come up with a ___________ to the problem of supplies?

B: Actually, they had no ___________ but to abandon the expedition.

5 decide | vary

A: To reach the top, we have a ___________ of routes to choose from.

B: Well, we'd better make a ___________ before we start climbing.

3 **Choose the correct words.**

1 Fortunately, the leader of the expedition wasn't lacking **from** / **in** experience.
2 There was something wrong **about** / **with** the poles, so I couldn't put up the tent.
3 The climbers had to seek shelter **from** / **in** the sudden snowstorm in a cave.
4 Warned **about** / **to** falling rocks on the mountain, I decided to wear a helmet.
5 While abseiling, I lost my balance and crashed **into** / **on** another climber.
6 For me, the purpose **to** / **of** mountaineering is to accomplish a difficult task.
7 We booked our holiday with a company that specialises **in** / **for** adventure travel.
8 To be honest, I wasn't very optimistic **about** / **with** getting to the top of the mountain.

8 GRAMMAR 2 | Review: countable/uncountable nouns, articles, quantifiers

→ Student's Book, page 85 → Grammar reference, Unit 8, Student's Book, page 156

1 **Choose the correct words.**

1 I said I would go rock climbing, but the truth **is** / **are**, I'm actually too scared to do it.
2 The wood that we collected in the forest **wasn't** / **weren't** dry enough to make a fire.
3 You shouldn't wear **this** / **these** new jeans to go abseiling; you might rip them.
4 I must say, the advice he gave us about climbing **have** / **has** been very useful.
5 While the sheep **was** / **were** being led up the mountain, one fell and hurt its leg.
6 Because the air on high mountains **is** / **are** thin, many climbers experience problems.
7 The accommodation I found online **don't** / **doesn't** seem too expensive.
8 Many pieces of equipment **was** / **were** damaged during the snowstorm.

2 **Complete the sentences with an article or quantifier. Write one word in each gap. If no word is needed, put a dash (–).**

1 How ___________ local knowledge did they use in order to reach the top of ___________ the mountain?
2 ___________ Swiss Alps, which are wonderful for hiking, are located east of ___________ Lake Geneva.
3 On our way up the mountain we got a ___________ tips from ___________ climber we didn't know.
4 Some mountains are actually volcanoes and ___________ example of this is Aconcagua in ___________ Argentina.
5 It takes a ___________ practice, but it's quite easy to work out the time by the position of ___________ sun.
6 There weren't ___________ routes to the summit, but we had to make ___________ choice and stick to it.
7 Tenzing Norgay was first employed as ___________ porter for earlier expeditions in ___________ 1930s.
8 A ___________ of the climbers were missing after the snowstorm and ___________ army was called in to help.

8 LISTENING | Sentence completion

→ Student's Book, page 84

1 Choose the correct words.

1 I **come** / **tend** to think that people who climb mountains are a bit reckless.
2 Equipment should be light but strong, which **makes** / **is** perfectly good sense to me.
3 Climbing without protective headgear **appears** / **seems** like a foolish thing to do.
4 Geology is an important subject and, to my **mind** / **view**, it should be taught at school.
5 **In person** / **Personally**, I agree that governments should sponsor expeditions.
6 My **mind** / **view** is that we should respect natural environments such as mountains.
7 Many people enjoy extreme sports, but **if** / **when** you ask me, I think they're crazy.
8 Lots of people say that hiking is a lot of fun, and I don't **disagree** / **deny** with that.

2 13 **Listen to the speakers and decide if they present a fact or express an opinion. Choose the correct option.**

1 fact / opinion
2 fact / opinion
3 fact / opinion
4 fact / opinion
5 fact / opinion
6 fact / opinion

3 14 **Listen to a student named Nina talking about mountains and mythology. Complete the sentences with a word or short phrase.**

Nina says it's **(1)** ______________________ to find connections between mountains and mythology.

Nina says in her talk that mountains don't disappear, but people, cities and entire **(2)** ______________________ do.

Nina understands why mountains were regarded as **(3)** ______________________ of mystery for ancient people.

It's Nina's opinion that one of the Olympus myths was actually a way to explain why **(4)** ______________________ couldn't be seen.

The Yeti is said by some to look like **(5)** ______________________ that is taller than a human being.

Nina agrees that people want to believe in something that is **(6)** ______________________ .

The Aztec warrior Popocatepetl returned after fighting **(7)** ______________________ .

According to legend, a Mexican volcano was created from **(8)** ______________________ one on top of the other.

8 SPEAKING | Discussion

→ Student's Book, page 86

1 Match to make sentences justifying opinions.

1 Skiing is the most exciting activity because ____
2 Rock climbing is the most tiring activity due to ____
3 Scrambling is the most dangerous activity because ____
4 Abseiling uses harnesses and ropes so ____

a) the fact you use every part of your body.
b) of the sharpness of the rocks.
c) it's the one I would probably do.
d) you can go quite fast.

2 Complete the sentences with the words in the box.

agree | ask | far | opinion (× 2) | personally | sense

1 I don't ____________ with the idea that mountain climbing is safe!
2 In my ____________ , skiing is only a sport for the rich.
3 As ____________ as I'm concerned, mountain climbing's too risky to try.
4 Actually, my ____________ is the exact opposite! I love climbing!
5 Rock climbing is dangerous? Yes, that makes ____________ to me.
6 If you ____________ me, abseiling is the most dangerous activity.
7 ____________ , I don't agree with you. I think mountains are quite dangerous.

3 **Rewrite the sentences in Exercise 2 with your own ideas. Use opinion phrases.**

1 ____________________
2 ____________________
3 ____________________
4 ____________________
5 ____________________
6 ____________________
7 ____________________

8 USE OF ENGLISH | Word formation

→ Student's Book, page 87

1 **Look at the gaps in the sentences and decide if they need a verb (V), an adjective (ADJ) or a noun (N).**

1 It was a ____________ climb to the summit and the mountaineers were both thrilled and exhausted when they reached it. ____
2 When we stopped to rest on a rock, the ____________ of the sun's rays made us feel very sleepy. ____
3 Zak wasn't chosen for the expedition because of his ____________, which could have put others at risk. ____
4 Several unique plants are known to ____________ in this region and we might be able to see some on the mountain. ____
5 The view from the summit was absolute ____________ and better than I could have possibly imagined. ____
6 Unless the skiers who are trapped on the southern slope are rescued soon, they will surely ____________. ____
7 Remember, guys: our greatest ____________ is our ability to work together as a team. Now, let's conquer that mountain! ____
8 As there was only a slight ____________ of rain that day, we loaded our backpacks and headed for the hills. ____
9 I'm sure there are age restrictions for abseiling and those who are too ____________ cannot take part. ____
10 If the river isn't very ____________, we will be able to cross it and continue our trek on the other side. ____

2 **Now complete the sentences in Exercise 1 with the words in the box in the correct form.**

death | depth | growth | length | mature | perfect | possible | strong | warm | youth

3 **Write a form of the word in capitals in each gap.**

The Lord of the Rings

Fans of *The Lord of the Rings* all agree that it is the greatest adventure story ever told. And who can disagree with them?

From the moment of Frodo's (**1**) ____________ from his home in the Shire to his (**2**) ____________ at Mount Doom, where he must destroy the Ring in order to save Middle Earth, the action never stops. Through mountains, snow, darkness and forests, Frodo and his friends face a (**3**) ____________ of evil characters who they must fight in order to survive. — **DEPART**, **ARRIVE**, **VARY**

At every corner, (**4**) ____________ awaits them and they can never be sure who is a friend and who is an enemy. The journey to Mount Doom isn't just a test of physical (**5**) ____________. It also tests their character and they develop a sense of (**6**) ____________ that pushes them on. — **DIE**, **STRONG**, **RESPONSIBLE**

Despite Frodo's (**7**) ____________ and, at times, what seems to be the (**8**) ____________ of the task, he succeeds. Mount Doom shakes violently as the Ring falls into it and is destroyed, and hope returns to Middle Earth. — **YOUNG**, **POSSIBLE**

WRITING | A letter / An email

→Student's Book, pages 88–89 →Writing reference, Student's Book, page 171

1 Read the email and then tick the things the writer has done.

1 ☐ used informal language
2 ☐ started and ended the email in the right way
3 ☐ referred to some news from Tom in the first paragraph
4 ☐ given useful information to answer Tom's question
5 ☐ asked Tom to reply
6 ☐ given news about her life

To: Tom
Subject: Summer holidays

Hi Tom,

Thanks for your email. It was great to hear from you! I'm glad your team won the match – scoring a goal must have been exciting!

You asked about a place in my country to visit and activities to do there. I know you love outdoor activities, so I would recommend that you fly to Krakow and then go to Ojcow National Park, 20 kilometres north of the city.

In the park, you can go on hiking and mountain biking trips with guides or you can explore the area by horse. Of course, you can walk round too! You should definitely visit the castle in Pieskow Skala – it's an amazing place, built in the 14th century. There are lots of prehistoric caves to visit, and some great places to eat.

After that, you could spend a few days in the city of Krakow. I can meet you there and show you around!

I hope that helps. Let me know how you get on!

Bye for now,

Kasia

2 Complete these phrases for starting and finishing an email.

1 ______________ [name],
2 ______________ for your email. It was great to ______________ from you!
3 I hope that ______________ .
4 ______________ me know if I can help with anything else.
5 ______________ soon!
6 Lots ______________ love,

3 Imagine you were writing to Tom about a place in your country and activities to do there. Write notes.

1 Invent some news of Tom's to comment on.

____

____

2 Say which place in your country you recommend.

____

____

3 Say why you think it's a good choice for Tom.

____

____

4 Say what activities you can do there.

____

____

4 Write the middle paragraphs of your email to Tom, using your notes from Exercise 3.

____

____

____

____

____

____

PROGRESS CHECK

1 Complete the sentences with the words in the box.

about | cliff | coast | from | in (× 2) | into | mountain | of (× 2) | path | slope | summit | volcano | waterfall | with

1 Although he was lacking ___________ experience, it didn't stop him from attempting to reach the ___________ with the other climbers.
2 The teacher warned the students about the dangers ___________ getting lost in the remote ___________ range.
3 The doctors were amazed that Julie only had a few bruises after she lost control of her boat and went over the ___________ and crashed ___________ the rocks in the river below.
4 The purpose ___________ this equipment is to detect whether a ___________ is active and might explode.
5 This company specialises ___________ tours for people who want to explore California and the west ___________ of the USA.
6 There was something wrong ___________ my skis, so I wasn't able to easily ski down the ___________ .
7 We were looking for shelter ___________ the rain when I fell over the edge of the ___________ and my climbing partner had to rescue me with a rope.
8 Hang on a minute. I think we're lost. I don't feel very optimistic ___________ this route. Are you sure we're on the right ___________ ?

2 Choose the best answer to complete each sentence.

1 Oh, no! My ski mask ___________ been stolen! Who would do such a thing?
a) is **b)** has **c)** was
2 In Switzerland, lost climbers are often found ___________ specially trained dogs.
a) by **b)** with **c)** from
3 Edmund Hillary was ___________ the title of 'Sir' for his accomplishment.
a) gave **b)** giving **c)** given
4 I suppose ski poles are made ___________ metal, but I don't really know.
a) by **b)** of **c)** with
5 Very ___________ climbers realised that the pass was blocked by snow.
a) little **b)** much **c)** few
6 ___________ media went crazy when the famous explorer arrived in the country.
a) The **b)** A **c)** –
7 How ___________ food do you think we'll need to carry with us?
a) many **b)** much **c)** few
8 I got some good advice from ___________ user on an online mountaineering site.
a) – **b)** a **c)** an

Cumulative progress 1 2 3 4 5 6 7 8 9 10 11 12

3 Write one word in each gap.

WHO GOT THERE FIRST?

High up on Mount Everest, there's a mystery waiting to **(1)** ___________ solved. It concerns two British mountaineers **(2)** ___________ died while attempting to conquer the mountain almost 30 years before Hillary and Tenzing. **(3)** ___________ men, George Mallory and Andrew Irvine, were last seen climbing on 8 June, 1924. They never returned to base camp and were presumed dead. Then, in 1999, Mallory's body was discovered **(4)** ___________ an American climber. The discovery raised a question: **(5)** ___________ Mallory and Irvine made it to the summit? Did they die on their way up **(6)** ___________ on their way down? One reliable **(7)** ___________ of evidence would be Mallory's camera. Experts at Kodak had said that **(8)** ___________ though the film would be old, they might still be able to develop it. Unfortunately, the camera has never been found, and until it is, the mystery will remain unsolved.

9 Music to my ears

READING | Gapped text

→Student's Book, pages 92–93

1 Read the article opposite and match paragraphs 1–7 to the descriptions (a–g).

a) First big break ____
b) An inspiration for future young musicians ____
c) Introduction ____
d) International stardom ____
e) How it all began ____
f) A musician for the people ____
g) The key year in Sheeran's career ____

2 Read the text again. Choose from the sentences A–G the one which fits each gap 1–6. There is one extra sentence which you do not need to use.

A This success lead to his first record deal in 2011.
B He also hasn't forgotten the people who made him famous.
C It's fair to say that Ed is now a household name, and not just in his native England.
D He showed an early talent for music, singing in a choir and starting to play the guitar before his fifth birthday.
E He never expected to be so famous, but he enjoys everything that it brings.
F Not bad for a man who was once homeless and busking on the streets of London.
G This was followed by three sold-out concerts in New York, where he was the lead act.

3 Find the highlighted words or phrases in the article and match them to the definitions below.

1 try to achieve ____________
2 very much respected and admired ____________
3 needed the help and support of others ____________
4 beginning to develop, showing signs of future success ____________
5 make someone think they are important ____________
6 admiring someone because of their achievements ____________
7 slept outside due to having no home and no money ____________
8 noticed ____________

FROM BUSKING TO THE BIG TIME

How did Ed Sheeran go from being a homeless musician to a world-famous singer? Here, we tell his rags-to-riches story.

Music News **By Ellie King, Music correspondent**

1 The singer and songwriter Ed Sheeran is only in his twenties, but already he's one of the most listened-to acts in the world, according to music-streaming site, Spotify. In one year, Sheeran's music was streamed and listened to more than 860 million times! [1 ______] The story of how he made it to the top is an interesting one.

2 Sheeran was born in the north of England in February 1991. [2 ______] By secondary school, he was writing and recording songs and music became his life. When he left school aged 16, he moved to London to pursue a career in music. There he played guitar in a folk band in the evenings and busked during the day. Ed's circumstances were not great. He often depended on other people for somewhere to spend the night and on occasion even slept rough.

3 Things started looking up in 2010. Sheeran went to Los Angeles and played open-mic nights all over the city. He was spotted by film star Jamie Foxx, who was so impressed that he offered him use of his recording studio. The following year, he released his EP *No. 5 Collaborations Project*, which sold over 7,000 copies in the first week and went to number two on the iTunes chart. [3 ______] He had arrived.

4 In 2012, Sheeran released his hugely successful album '+' ('plus') and won several prestigious music awards, including two Brit awards. Not only that, but Taylor Swift contacted him after hearing his music and he made a guest appearance on her album *Red*. He spent most of 2013 touring the US as her opening act. [4 ______]

5 Since then, it has been one success after another. His 2014 follow-up album 'X' ('multiply'), charted at number one in both the UK and USA and won the Brit Award for British Album of the Year. With over two million sales worldwide, it is one of the biggest-selling albums of the decade. [5 ______]

6 Sheeran hasn't let success go to his head. Despite hitting the big time, he still has time for others. He has helped to raise money for a variety of charities, including the 2014 Band Aid 30 project for the Ebola crisis in Africa. [6 ______] In 2015, he surprised a fan in a Canadian shopping mall by singing a duet with her. You can check out this special moment on YouTube.

7 Ed's story is a lesson for all budding musicians. It is a story of dedication and persistence as well as talent. So if you are currently busking in the streets or playing concerts for free, don't give up. Fame could be waiting for you just around the corner.

9 GRAMMAR 1 | Reported speech

→ Student's Book, page 94 → Grammar reference, Unit 9, Student's Book, page 156

1 Choose the correct words to complete the reported speech.

1 'I can read the notes.'
He **said** / **told** me he could read the notes.

2 'How many stages will there be at the festival?'
He asked me how many **will the stages be** / **stages there would be** at the festival.

3 'I certainly didn't take your maracas!'
She **denied taking my** / **denied me to take** maracas.

4 'Did you learn to play the guitar at music school?'
He asked me **had I learnt** / **whether I had learnt** to play the guitar at music school.

5 'You should practise more.'
She **advised me to practise** / **suggested me practising** more.

6 'I heard you on the radio yesterday!'
She said she had heard me on the radio the day **before** / **previous**.

2 Read the direct speech then complete the gaps in the reported speech. Use the reporting verbs in the box and any other words you need.

claimed | promised | refused | suggested | warned

1 'Don't lose the concert tickets!'
He ______________________ to lose the concert tickets.

2 'I'll help you with the recording.'
She ______________________ me with the recording.

3 'Why don't you audition for the show?'
He ______________________ audition for the show.

4 'No, I won't sing in front of an audience!'
He ______________________ in front of an audience.

5 'I know who the singer's new girlfriend is!'
She ______________________ the identity of the singer's new girlfriend.

3 Read the dialogue below. Then write one word in each gap in the article opposite.

Seth: What inspired you to become a singer, Kion?
Kion: Basically it's because I wanted to be famous.
Seth: I see. And are you happy with your fame?
Kion: Of course! I've been having the time of my life!
Seth: So what's next for you, Kion?
Kion: I'm going to be in a film next month.
Seth: Have you had any acting experience?
Kion: No, but how hard can it be, right?
Seth: It'll be a piece of cake, I'm sure. Well, good luck with that, Kion.

An interview with Kion Pratt
■ by Seth Moss

I caught up with teen singing sensation Kion Pratt in London last week. I asked him what (**1**) ___________ inspired him to become a singer. He (**2**) ___________ that it was because he wanted to be famous. Next I asked him (**3**) ___________ he was happy with (**4**) ___________ fame and he (**5**) ___________ me that he was. He said that he had (**6**) ___________ having the time of his life. My next question was about his immediate future. I asked him what was next and he said he was going to be in a film the (**7**) ___________ month. I asked him if he (**8**) ___________ any acting experience. He said he hadn't and wondered how hard it (**9**) ___________ be. I assured him it (**10**) ___________ be a piece of cake and wished him good luck.

9 VOCABULARY | Topic vocabulary | Phrasal verbs | Word formation

→ Student's Book, page 95 → Vocabulary reference, Student's Book, page 166

1 Write the missing words to complete the idioms.

a) blow your own t _ _ _ _ _ _
b) change your t _ _ _
c) d _ _ _ up support
d) face the m _ _ _ _
e) fit as a f _ _ _ _ _
f) make a s _ _ _ and dance about
g) play it by e _ _
h) ring a b _ _ _

2 **Match the idioms a–h in Exercise 1 to the definitions below.**

1 boast about something ____
2 very well ____
3 accept the punishment or criticism ____
4 sound familiar ____
5 increase interest in something ____
6 completely change your opinion ____
7 make something seem more important than it really is ____
8 deal with a situation as it develops ____

3 **Match to make sentences. Use the words in italics to help you.**

1 I don't think I can *take* ____
2 The rock festival is *coming* ____
3 Vanessa had to *drop* ____
4 Without *giving* ____
5 If you don't *go* ____
6 It's too bad you were *knocked* ____
7 After his win, Max *went* ____
8 We're thinking of *putting* ____

a) *out* early in the competition; better luck next time.
b) *on* the music and the stage settings; it's too much.
c) *away* too much, I can tell you the prize this year is going to be huge!
d) *on to* record an album and host his own popular TV show.
e) *up* and I'm really looking forward to it.
f) *on* the show at a theatre in town instead of at the school.
g) *in for* the TV song contest, you might miss your big opportunity.
h) *out of* music school as it clashed with her schedule.

4 **Complete the sentences with the correct form of the words in brackets.**

1 She's the most talented ____________ (**violin**) in the world because she's such a ____________ (**perfect**).
2 He made his name as a ____________ (**journal**) when he wrote about bands being exploited by ____________ (**account**) and managers.
3 Being an extreme ____________ (**optimism**), Becky applied to be on the next series of *X Factor* fully convinced that she was the best ____________ (**application**).
4 After a while, the ____________ (**contest**) were led to the stage by an ____________ (**assist**) to the producer.
5 He may be a famous ____________ (**guitar**), but he's rude and disliked by his staff, whom he treats like ____________ (**serve**).
6 When the throat ____________ (**special**) arrived to examine the opera singer, an ____________ (**attend**) took him to her apartment on the tenth floor.

9 GRAMMAR 2 | Indirect questions

→ Student's Book, page 97 → Grammar reference, Unit 9, Student's Book, page 157

1 **Choose the correct phrases.**

1 I'd ________________________ what you did before you became a singer.
a) wonder if you could tell us **b)** like to know **c)** grateful if you told me
2 Could you tell us what ________________________ ?
a) is the life on tour like **b)** does the life on tour like **c)** life on tour is like
3 ________________________ you could sign a few autographs for our listeners?
a) Do you think **b)** Do you wonder whether **c)** I wonder
4 Could you tell us ________________________ the tour?
a) whether are you enjoying **b)** are you enjoying **c)** whether you are enjoying

2 **Rewrite the sentences correctly.**

1 Do you know which band does perform first?
____
2 I wonder could you tell me who produced your album.
____
3 Could you tell me whether do you like touring?
____
4 I like you tell us who designs your costumes.
____
5 I am grateful if you tell us when you practise.
____

9 LISTENING | Sentence completion

→ Student's Book, page 96

1 15 **Listen to a girl called Lia talking about her band. Choose the best set of notes.**

A

one performance
14
Manchester
drummer
friends and neighbour
played hits
bad original songs, lyrics not good

B

Mr Strummer, music teacher
a few years ago
in Manchester everyone wanted to be in a band
electric guitar, bass, neighbour singer, drummer
wrote songs with bass player

2 Answer the questions about the notes.

1 Which notes provide the best summary of what the speaker said?

____

2 Which notes contain irrelevant information? Give an example.

____

3 Which notes would take too long to write? Why?

____

3 16 **Listen to the complete talk about Lia's band. Complete the sentences with a word or short phrase.**

Lia's band performed live only **(1)** ______________ .

Lia was the **(2)** ______________ in the band.

The songs Lia wrote with the bass player were not **(3)** ______________ .

Lia had to take her drums to rehearsals in a **(4)** ______________ .

The name of Lia's band was **(5)** ______________ .

Lia's cousin knew someone who could play **(6)** ______________ .

When the band set up their gear, they looked **(7)** ______________ .

The band's performance at the café that night was **(8)** ______________ .

9 SPEAKING | Photo task

→ Student's Book, page 98

1 Look at the photo and choose the correct words.

1 She **might** / **perhaps** be in a band.
2 She **maybe** / **could be** having a music lesson.
3 **Maybe** / **Might be** she's learning to play the drums.
4 **Could** / **Perhaps** she's at a music shop because she wants to buy the drums.
5 It's difficult **to tell** / **tell** but maybe she's at a recording studio.
6 It's not **fully** / **totally** clear, but one **possible** / **possibility** is that she's at a rehearsal.
7 I'm not really **sure** / **positive**, but I **understand** / **imagine** she might be at an audition.

2 **Look at the two photos and complete the notes.**

1 Who might the people be? ____________________
2 What might they be doing? ____________________
3 Why might they be doing it? ____________________
4 Where might they be? ____________________

3 **Describe the photos, saying how you think the people are feeling. Talk for one minute.**

9 USE OF ENGLISH | Multiple-choice cloze

→ Student's Book, page 99

1 **Choose the correct answers. Use the words in italics to help you.**

1 We need to ____________________ *support* for the show or no-one will be there!
a) look up **b)** bring up **c)** drum up

2 I know you're worried about telling the teacher, but it's time to ____________________ *the music* and tell her what's happened.
a) listen to **b)** read **c)** face

3 I know you're upset, but I don't think you need to *make a song and* ____________________ *about it*!
a) dance **b)** tune **c)** bell

4 I'm glad you're better! You look *as fit as a* ____________________ now.
a) trumpet **b)** fiddle **c)** bell

5 Before I went on stage, I ____________________ *butterflies in my stomach*.
a) had **b)** did **c)** felt

6 We were all nervous, but our singer was *as* ____________________ *as a cucumber*.
a) cold **b)** cool **c)** freezing

7 What made you *change your* ____________________ about performing?
a) song **b)** music **c)** tune

8 People won't like you if you ____________________ *your own trumpet*.
a) blow **b)** hold **c)** use

2 **Choose the correct word for each gap.**

There have been claims that some contestants who **(1)** ____________ in for TV singing contests are professionals and not, as they are supposed to be, amateurs. Not so long ago, I heard of a girl band who **(2)** ____________ for a talent show, but actually had a long history of TV appearances and record releases in the country they came from. It turns out they were actually **(3)** ____________ performers – in fact, they were so professional that they had previously been on **(4)** ____________ .

It's thought the show's producer knew the situation. Of course, from the point of view of TV ratings, producers have to think about the show they are **(5)** ____________ on for the public. But is it fair on contestants who are amateurs and are knocked **(6)** ____________ early because they are competing against professionals? And if professional contestants go **(7)** ____________ to win, are they robbing amateurs of possible success?

Viewers of TV talent shows are on the **(8)** ____________ of their seats, waiting anxiously to see if their favourite act will win. But, are they in with a fair chance?

	a)	b)	c)	d)
1	**a)** took	**b)** ask	**c)** go	**d)** do
2	**a)** auditioned	**b)** practised	**c)** appeared	**d)** tried
3	**a)** managed	**b)** accomplished	**c)** effective	**d)** qualified
4	**a)** tour	**b)** course	**c)** travel	**d)** road
5	**a)** presenting	**b)** showing	**c)** placing	**d)** putting
6	**a)** off	**b)** down	**c)** by	**d)** out
7	**a)** at	**b)** to	**c)** on	**d)** up
8	**a)** last	**b)** edge	**c)** bottom	**d)** end

WRITING | A review

→ Student's Book, pages 100–101 → Writing reference, Student's Book, page 170

1 Match to make sentences containing the exam skill advice.

1 Some writing tasks ____
2 When you write an exam task, ____
3 If you are writing a review for young people, ____

a) think about what interests them.
b) have a particular target reader in mind.
c) you should think about your target audience.

2 Read the exam task and decide if the sentences are T (True) or F (False).

1 The writer has included an introduction. T / F
2 The writer doesn't give any information about the programme (e.g. who created it, when it started, etc.). T / F
3 The writer talks about the positive and negative aspects of the programme. T / F
4 The writer gives a recommendation. T / F
5 The writer has considered his target audience in the text. T / F
6 The writer is a fan of the show he is reviewing. T / F

You see this advert in an English-language magazine for young people:

Reviews wanted!

Music programmes

We're looking for reviews of music programmes on TV. Your review should include information about the type of programme, when it was created and other relevant information. Would you recommend this programme to other people your age?

The best reviews will be published in next month's magazine.

Write your **review**.

'American Idol': a waste of time?

Are you looking for an interesting music programme featuring exciting new music performers? If so, 'American Idol' might be for you.

The series 'American Idol' started in 2002, and was well-received at first. It is a reality show that aims to find new recording artists and it was created by Simon Fuller, based on the British series 'Pop Idol'. Members of the public vote which contestants should stay on the show and the winner gets a record deal.

It is true that some very talented singers such as Carrie Underwood or Jennifer Hudson have been discovered through the show. However, in my opinion the voting isn't always fair, so the best contestants don't always win. The focus seems to be about drama and tension rather than talent. In addition, I feel the variety of singers is very limited, so they all end up sounding the same and I feel the programme is too commercial.

I personally wouldn't recommend 'American Idol' to older teenage music fans. I believe you can find more interesting singers online. However, younger teens might enjoy it.

Sam

3 Look at the exam task in Exercise 2 again and complete the paragraph plan.

	Purpose	Notes
Paragraph 1	introduce the programme, and engage and interest the reader	
Paragraph 2/3	over two paragraphs, describe the type of programme, when it was created and any other useful information	
Paragraph 4	say if you recommend the programme or not and briefly explain why	

PROGRESS CHECK

1 Complete each line with the correct form of the word in brackets or a word from the box.

blow | drop | drum | give | go (× 2) | make | ring

1 **A:** How's your throat? Have you been to see the ___________ (**special**) yet?
B: Let's not ___________ a song and dance about it; I'm sure it's fine.
2 **A:** John Smith is a great music ___________ (**journal**). Have you read any of his articles?
B: I'm not sure who you mean. The name doesn't ___________ a bell.
3 **A:** Celine has been trying to ___________ up support for the youth music festival.
B: I know. She's the ___________ (**assist**) to the producer, so she has to.
4 **A:** My friend at ATV studios told me which ___________ (**contest**) is going to win.
B: Well, don't ___________ it away! I want to watch the final on Saturday!
5 **A:** What if I ___________ in for one of those TV singing contests? Do you think I could win?
B: You're such an ___________ (**optimism**), Fred! You can't even sing!
6 **A:** My favourite performer had to ___________ out of the talent show.
B: The ___________ (**violin**)? Why? Was she sick?
7 **A:** Honestly, I do think I'm the best ___________ (**guitar**) in the school band.
B: Maybe, but it's not nice to ___________ your own trumpet, Jimmy.
8 **A:** Did anyone on that show ever ___________ on to become a popular artist?
B: Yes. A classical ___________ (**piano**) was hugely successful.

2 Choose the correct words or phrases.

1 I saw Mike and he **told / told to** me that he was going to record an album.
2 The interviewer asked the singer who **did she enjoy / she enjoyed** listening to.
3 Helen said she was excited about going to the music festival **this / that** day.
4 The manager refused **to say / that he said** anything about the opera singer.
5 Katy said she had downloaded a few songs **two days before / before two days**.
6 I'd be grateful if you **tell / could tell** me about your new song.
7 Could you tell me when **is your next concert / your next concert is**?
8 I wonder if you know where **I can buy / can I buy** tickets for the concert.
9 **I'd / I** like to know who will produce your next studio album.
10 Can you tell us why **did you leave / you left** the band?

Cumulative progress 1 2 3 4 5 6 7 8 9 10 11 12

3 Write a form of the word in capitals in each gap.

THE BOY BAND PHENOMENON

Groups like *One Direction* and *The Wanted* are the latest in a long line of (**1**) ___________ successful all-male music groups known as boy bands. The continued (**2**) ___________ of boy bands is due to a winning formula: take five or so (**3**) ___________ young males, teach them to sing and dance, write some catchy tunes for them, and find (**4**) ___________ to advise on hair, clothes and attitude.

As long as the (**5**) ___________ between the members are strong and the band produces hits (**6**) ___________, all is well. Sometimes, though, one member becomes more popular. When this happens, dreams of a solo career are never far away. The other band members begin to feel (**7**) ___________ and, before too long, the 'star' leaves. The band breaks up because it is (**8**) ___________ to continue without him.

The fans are sad, but only until a new boy band comes along to take its place.

REMARKABLE
POPULAR
ATTRACT
CONSULT
FRIEND
REGULAR
SECURE
ABLE

10 Run till you drop

READING | Open questions

→Student's Book, pages 102–103

1 **Read the questions in Exercise 2 and choose synonyms from the box for the underlined words and phrases.**

challenging | clothes | enjoy | every 10–15 minutes | exhausting huge boulders | initial | runners | sections | stop

1 ______________ ______________
2 ______________ ______________
3 ______________ ______________
4 ______________
5 ______________ ______________ ______________

2 **Read the text opposite then write a short answer for each question. Use a maximum of four words.**

1 How many athletes took part in the first marathon?
____
2 Why are some parts of the route so tiring?
____
3 What happens to the large rocks in one section, making it difficult to get through?
____
4 What should your outfit not do?
____
5 What do some participants frequently pause to appreciate?
____

3 **Find words in the text which match the definitions below.**

1 extremely beautiful, awesome (paragraph 2) ______________
2 gradually, consistently (paragraph 2) ______________
3 most difficult (paragraph 3) ______________
4 at a sharp inclination or gradient (paragraph 3) ______________
5 perspire, produce liquid on your skin when you are hot (paragraph 4) ______________
6 make an organised or determined attempt to do something difficult (paragraph 4) ______________
7 weak or ill because you have lost a lot of water from your body (paragraph 4) ______________
8 difficult, needing a lot of physical effort (paragraph 5) ______________

The Great Wall Marathon

Do you love running and sightseeing? Well, there are some amazing events where you can combine both – the Great Wall Marathon is one of them.

At 7,200 km long, the Great Wall of China is one of the new wonders of the world, with breathtaking views. In 1998 Søren Rasmussen came up with the idea of organising a Great Wall marathon. Rasmussen and two running experts chose a route along part of the Great Wall. The marathon has taken place annually in May since 1999. In the initial event, just 292 runners participated but numbers have gone up steadily – in 2015 there were 2,500 runners from over 60 countries.

The Great Wall Marathon is considered to be one of the toughest in the world. The portion of the route that is actually on the Great Wall includes two exhausting up and down sections about 8 km long with 5,164 steps. It's such a steep climb in parts that it's hard to walk up – never mind run! The weather is hot and humid, with temperatures of around 30°C, but it can be hotter. Part of the route passes through a dry river bed with huge boulders. Runners who arrive there later in the day find it challenging because the boulders have become so hot that it's like running through a sauna – this part of the route has been nicknamed 'the Gobi Desert'.

The organisers offer some useful tips for runners. It's best to wear short-sleeved tops and have light-coloured clothes that don't absorb moisture because you will sweat a lot in the heat. A hat is also a good idea and sunscreen is essential. Your preparation should include plenty of training on stairs and slopes so you can tackle the hills on the route. Most importantly, it's hot so you must remember to drink regularly during the marathon. If you don't drink enough water, you run the risk of becoming seriously dehydrated.

So who does the marathon? Surprisingly, the marathon attracts both extreme competitors and people who want to run for fun or simply do something different. Some runners stop every 10–15 minutes to take photos, chat to the locals and enjoy the scenery! If the thought of doing such a strenuous marathon horrifies you, then you can do a half marathon or an 8 km fun run instead.

10 GRAMMAR 1 | Result clauses: *so, such, too, enough*

→ Student's Book, page 104 → Grammar reference, Unit 10, Student's Book, page 158

1 Choose the correct answers.

1 I think doing a marathon would be ____ much for me. **a)** so **b)** too **c)** enough
2 I haven't got ____ time to train for the marathon. **a)** such **b)** too **c)** enough
3 The race was ____ exciting that I watched it from start to finish. **a)** so **b)** such a **c)** too
4 There were ____ entrants for the fun run that they were split into three groups. **a)** so many **b)** too many **c)** not enough
5 We had ____ terrible time that we're never competing again. **a)** so **b)** such a **c)** too
6 Tom had done ____ training that he achieved a new personal best time. **a)** such a **b)** such a lot of **c)** such
7 I'm very unfit – even 5 km is ____ far for me to run! **a)** enough **b)** so **c)** too
8 The sun was ____ hot during the race that I got sunburnt. **a)** so **b)** so much **c)** too

2 Tick the correct sentences. Underline the mistakes in the other sentences and correct them.

1 We stayed up such late that we were tired the next day. ____________
2 I drank water enough during the race so I didn't get dehydrated. ____________
3 I've run too many marathons in so many different countries that I'm becoming an expert! ____________
4 I've got money enough to pay for the entry fee – luckily it isn't too expensive. ____________
5 Kate has already been running today; it's so much to expect her to do more. ____________
6 Jamie is strong enough to lift all those heavy weights. ____________

3 Write one word in each gap.

City to Surf is an annual fun run in Sydney, Australia. The route goes from the city centre to Bondi Beach. It's 14 km long and there's only one big hill, so it's not **(1)** ____________ difficult for me **(2)** ____________ do. It's now **(3)** ____________ a popular race **(4)** ____________ over 80,000 people participate every year! There are **(5)** ____________ many people that there are five different starting points. That way, there's **(6)** ____________ space **(7)** ____________ everyone to run comfortably. Although some elite athletes do take part, most people do it for fun and don't take it **(8)** ____________ seriously – some people even walk instead of running and there are a lot of wheelchair participants. Many entrants wear fancy dress and it's **(9)** ____________ a colourful event **(10)** ____________ it attracts huge crowds to cheer people on.

10 VOCABULARY | Topic vocabulary | Word formation | Idioms

→ Student's Book, page 105 → Vocabulary reference, Unit 10, Student's Book, page 166

1 Complete the puzzle and find the hidden word.

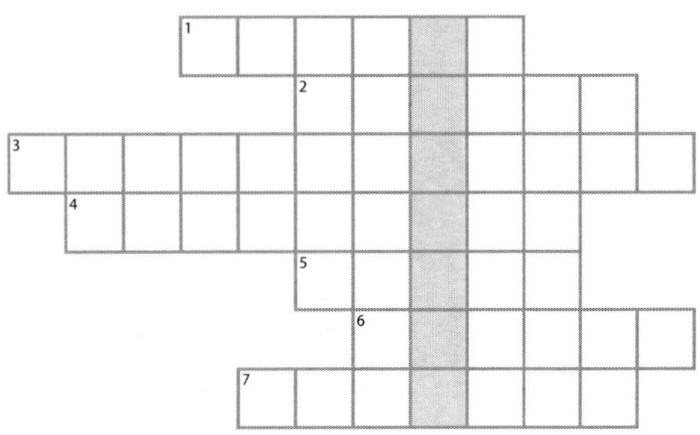

1 We had a great team of ____________ at the marathon to provide first aid and help people with minor injuries.
2 The event takes place over five days, and Sam was the ____________ on the second and third days. Perhaps he'll win.
3 There were over 6,000 ____________ in the Fun Run – that's more entrants than last year.
4 I'm proud to be a ____________ of our local football team – I never miss a match.
5 We've been training hard with our ____________ this week to get ready for the big game on Saturday.
6 Suzie came first in the competition, so she was the ____________ .
7 We are looking for a ____________ to pay for us to take part in the marathon next year.

2 **Write a form of the word in capitals in each gap.**

1 This picture is too small to see, we need to ___________ it. **LARGE**
2 The route is very short, let's ___________ it by another 5 km. **LONG**
3 Fitness and ___________ are two things you need to run a marathon. **STRONG**
4 Nobody is sure of the exact ___________ of the water, but it is certainly more than 1 km to the bottom. **DEEP**
5 The path isn't very ___________ here, so runners can't run side by side. **WIDTH**
6 What is the ___________ of that huge hill you have to run up in the event? **HIGH**
7 The shelf is too high to reach, you need to ___________ it by at least a metre. **LOW**

3 **Complete the sentences with the expressions in the box.**

hit the ground running | run a mile | run off my feet | run the risk running around in circles | running start | trying to run | up and running

1 We were really busy in the shop yesterday. I was ___________ .
2 I was very active yesterday, but I didn't achieve much. Basically, I was ___________ .
3 If you don't leave now, you ___________ of missing the bus.
4 Jackie has just started the job, but she's already been really successful. I'd say she's ___________ .
5 I really don't like spiders – when I see one I ___________ .
6 Mark has just started learning the guitar and already plans to win a talent show. He's ___________ before he can walk!
7 We need to start planning now if we want to get the business ___________ by the end of the year.
8 They did well in the first round of the competition. I think they got off to a ___________ .

10 GRAMMAR 2 | Conditionals (2): third conditional

→ Student's Book, page 107 → Grammar reference, Unit 10, Student's Book, page 158

1 **Complete the text using the correct form of the verbs in brackets.**

Jessica Ennis-Hill is a British track athlete and Olympic gold medallist. When she was ten years old, her parents took her to a major track event. If they (**1**) ___________ (**not take**) her, she (**2**) ___________ (**might not become**) interested in athletics. Jessica was very good at running and she won her first athletics prize there. She (**3**) ___________ (**not win**) the prize if she (**4**) ___________ (**not be**) so fast! She also met her trainer Toni Minichiello there – he's coached her since she was 13 years old. If she (**5**) ___________ (**not go**) to the event, she (**6**) ___________ (**not meet**) him. Luckily, he's still her trainer now since she (**7**) ___________ (**might not do**) so well if she (**8**) ___________ (**have**) a different trainer. In 2005 she was one of the runners-up at the Commonwealth Games – she (**9**) ___________ (**might win**) if she (**10**) ___________ (**run**) faster in the track events. By 2009 she had improved, and in 2012 she won a gold medal at the London Olympics.

2 **Complete the third conditional sentences.**

1 They loved running so they joined the sports club. If they ___________ ___________ .
2 I couldn't take part in the race because I forgot my sports clothes. If ___________ ___________ .
3 I spent three hours training every day and I won the race. I might ___________ ___________ .
4 Lucy forgot to give me the entry form so I didn't know about the fun run. If ___________ ___________ .

10 LISTENING | Multiple choice (single extract)

→Student's Book, page 106

1 17 **Listen to the start of an interview and complete the extract by writing a short phrase in each gap.**

Mia: Jonnie is one of **(1)** ______________ amputee sprinters in the world in the 100 m race. In 2012 he set a new **(2)** ______________ for the 100 m of 10.85 seconds, which beat the previous record of 10.91 seconds. Later that year, he won **(3)** ______________ at the Paralympic Games in London. Paralympic Games, as you know, are the Olympic Games for athletes with physical and intellectual disabilities.

2 **Use the extract above to help you choose the correct answer for question 1 in Exercise 3.** ____

3 18 **Listen to the complete interview about Jonnie Peacock and choose the best answers (A, B or C).**

1 What did Jonnie Peacock do in 2012?
- **A** He became the fastest sprinter in the world.
- **B** He won several gold medals in 100-metre races.
- **C** He broke the previous world record.

2 What happened after Jonnie's leg had to be amputated?
- **A** He spent months in a wheelchair.
- **B** He started using a prosthetic leg.
- **C** He knew he would never have a normal life.

3 Jonnie became interested in athletics
- **A** after going to the Paralympic Games in China.
- **B** because he couldn't play other sports like football and rugby.
- **C** after attending a special Paralympic event.

4 Who was at the international training camp?
- **A** There was a mix of athletes with and without disabilities.
- **B** There were only 10 able-bodied athletes.
- **C** There were no able-bodied athletes.

5 As a result of winning a Paralympic gold medal, Jonnie
- **A** decided to become a role model for younger athletes.
- **B** became very famous in Britain and appeared on television.
- **C** achieved his dream of being the fastest Paralympian runner ever.

4 18 **Listen again and check your answers.**

10 SPEAKING | Interview

→Student's Book, page 108

1 19 **Complete the answers with the words in the box. Then listen and check.**

actually | counts | funny | honest | sadly | sounds | though

a) No, ____________ . I'd love to ____________ . If I could meet any famous sportsperson, I'd love to meet the swimmer Ellie Simmons. She's my sports hero.

b) It's ____________ you should ask that – I've just started running twice a week with a friend. We go to the local park. I wouldn't enjoy running in a gym because I think running on a treadmill must be really boring.

c) No. To be ____________ , most people I know aren't very sporty. I'd like to do a half marathon one day – it ____________ like fun.

d) Well, I haven't won a competition, but I won the 400-metre race at our school Sports Day last year, if that ____________ .

e) Yes, ____________ . We had a sponsored run at school last term to raise money to buy sports equipment. We ran in fancy dress and we had a great time! I'd definitely do one again.

2 **Match the answers in Exercise 1 to these questions.**

1 Have you ever won a sports competition? ____
2 Do you run regularly in a park or gym? If so, which do you think is better? ____
3 Have you ever taken part in a sponsored run? Would you like to? ____
4 Has anybody you know ever run a marathon or half marathon? ____
5 Have you ever seen a famous sportsperson in a live event? ____

3 **Write your own answers to the questions in Exercise 2.**

1 ____________________
2 ____________________
3 ____________________
4 ____________________
5 ____________________

10 USE OF ENGLISH | Sentence transformation

→Student's Book, page 109

1 **Complete the conditional sentences with the correct form of the verbs in brackets.**

1 If you ____________ (**train**) before school, you'd have more free time in the evening.
2 If you ____________ (**run**) every day, you get stronger.
3 You'll see lots of famous sports stars if you ____________ (**go**) to the marathon.
4 You ____________ (**win**) the race if you hadn't fallen over.
5 If you sponsor me, I ____________ (**be**) more motivated to do the run next week!
6 If it ____________ (**rain**) heavily, we wouldn't have done the fun run.
7 You ____________ (**enjoy**) it if you went running in the park with me.
8 People are healthier if they ____________ (**do**) sport regularly.

2 **Add the sentence numbers from Exercise 1 in the correct place.**

Conditional	Use	Sentences
zero	general truths and scientific facts	___ ___
first	real or likely situations now, generally or in the future	___ ___
second	hypothetical, impossible or unlikely situations now, generally or in the future	___ ___
third	hypothetical situations in the past	___ ___

3 **Look at Exercise 4. Which questions test your knowledge of conditionals?**

___ ___

4 **Complete the second sentence so it has a similar meaning to the first. Do not change the word given. Use two to five words, including the word given.**

1 The day was so cold that we didn't go outside. **SUCH**
It was ____________________ that we didn't go outside.
2 How long is the route that you run? **THE**
What ____________________ the route you run?
3 The running top was too small for me. **ENOUGH**
The running top ____________________ for me.
4 Make sure you drink enough water or there's a chance you'll get dehydrated. **RUN**
If you don't drink enough water, ____________________ getting dehydrated.
5 Sara didn't take part in the race because her leg was broken. **NOT**
If ____________________ her leg, she would have taken part in the race.
6 The steps aren't low enough for people to run up them. **HIGH**
The steps ____________________ to run up them.

WRITING | A story

→Student's Book, pages 110–111 →Writing reference, Student's Book, page 173

1 Match to make sentences containing the exam skill advice.

1 The 'plot' of a story is ____
2 Successful plots in short stories are ____
3 Unsuccessful plots in short stories are ____

a) simple, with a few main characters and a few key events.
b) complicated, with too many characters and too much action.
c) the events that happen in it.

2 Read the exam task and the story and decide if the sentences are T (True) or F (False).

Story competition!

We will publish the winning story in our magazine. Your story must begin with the sentence:

It was an important race with a prize of $5,000!

Your story must include:

- a running race
- an unusual event

Write your story.

Write your answer in **140–190** words.

Tom was waiting at the start line, his heart thumping fast. 'I can win, I know I can. And I know exactly what I'll do with the money,' he thought. It was an important race with a prize of $5,000!

'You'd better not win,' his friend Harry said angrily. 'I need that prize!'

After an hour, Tom was in second place. Harry and the other runners were a long way behind him. Only Richard, in front of him now. 'Think of the money,' Tom repeated silently as he ran. He was exhausted, but he ran faster and faster. Just before the finishing line, he passed Richard – Tom had won! The money was his!

After the race, he went over to Harry, who was with his sister, Catriona. They both looked disappointed. 'What do you want?' Harry asked. 'You knew how important that race was for me!'

Tom smiled. 'Yes, I did. Listen, Harry. I knew you weren't fast enough to win. If I hadn't taken part, Richard would have won.' Then he turned to Catriona. 'I didn't do it for me. The prize money's for you. Now you can get that operation you need!'

1 The prize money for the race is fifty thousand dollars. **T / F**
2 Tom's friend, Harry, is happy that Tom is participating in the race. **T / F**
3 Tom comes first in the race and Harry comes second. **T / F**
4 Tom ran the race because he knew Harry wouldn't win. **T / F**
5 Harry wanted the prize money so he could have an operation. **T / F**
6 Tom gives the money to Harry's sister for an operation. **T / F**

3 Tick the things the student did NOT do in their story.

1 I've made sure my story mentions a running race and an unusual event. ☐
2 I've written at least four main paragraphs. ☐
3 I've included some direct speech. ☐
4 I've written between 140 and 190 words. ☐
5 I've given my story a good title. ☐
6 I've created an appropriate and interesting plot with a good ending. ☐
7 I began my story with the correct sentence. ☐

4 Think of a good title for the student's story. ____________________

PROGRESS CHECK

1 Complete the words in the sentences. The first letter is there to help you.

1 There were lots of m__________ at the marathon to give first aid and treat injuries.
2 Mum's really scared of mice – she runs a m__________ if she sees one!
3 The race route includes a dangerously narrow path – we need to w__________ it to make it safe for runners.
4 John hit the g__________ running when he started his new school and made friends very quickly.
5 Lots of football s__________ are prepared to travel to other countries to watch their favourite teams play.
6 You can't run through the river. It's too d__________ – the water will be over your head!
7 I've been really busy today. In fact, I've been run off my f__________ .
8 Sam is a f__________ for the organisation. Last year he got donations of over £5,000 for them.

2 Complete the second sentence so it has a similar meaning to the first. Do not change the word given. Use two to five words, including the word given.

1 We couldn't see the race because of the large number of people in the crowd. **MANY**
There ______________________ in the crowd that we couldn't see the race.
2 We didn't win the championship because the other team was better. **MIGHT**
If we had been better than the other team, ______________________ the championship.
3 Chris was too weak to finish the race. **STRONG**
Chris was ______________________ the race.
4 Everyone watched the event because it was so exciting. **AN**
It ______________________ that everyone watched it.
5 I didn't beat my personal best time in the marathon because I didn't feel well. **FELT**
If ______________________, I could have beaten my personal best time in the marathon.
6 Unfortunately, I didn't get a place in the marathon because so many people applied. **TOO**
Unfortunately, ______________________ for me to get a place in the marathon.

Cumulative progress 1 2 3 4 5 6 7 8 9 10 11 12

3 Choose the correct word or phrase for each gap.

McFarland, USA is a 2015 sports drama film which **(1)** ____ on the true story of a cross-country running team at McFarland High School in California.

When Jim White moved from Idaho to McFarland, he started a new job at a high school as a life science and PE teacher. He convinced the school principal **(2)** ____ him start a cross-country running team after noticing that some of the students were good runners. Jim started training the team and decided to run the **(3)** ____ of entering them in the state championships. At their first event, the team came last because they hadn't done **(4)** ____ training. Jim was convinced that if they **(5)** ____ more, they would have done better. At the second event, the team managed to qualify for the finals. Jim worked hard to help the team increase their strength and stamina. The team trained **(6)** ____ hard that they improved tremendously. On the day of the finals, everyone in McFarland went to support their team. With the **(7)** ____ cheering wildly, the McFarland team won and became state champions! **(8)** ____ being offered a better job, Jim stayed at McFarland High School and continued to train the running team.

	A	B	C	D
1	**A** based	**B** has based	**C** is based	**D** had been based
2	**A** to let	**B** let	**C** letting	**D** lets
3	**A** difficulty	**B** risk	**C** challenge	**D** danger
4	**A** too	**B** enough	**C** so many	**D** such
5	**A** train	**B** would have trained	**C** had trained	**D** have trained
6	**A** such	**B** such a	**C** so	**D** enough
7	**A** referees	**B** participants	**C** sponsors	**D** supporters
8	**A** Although	**B** Despite	**C** However	**D** While

11 All in a day's work

READING | Multiple matching

Student's Book, pages 114–115

1 **Read paragraphs A and B in the article opposite, and find close synonyms for these words and phrases.**

A

1 internationally ________________

2 pleased, happy ________________

B

3 unfamiliar, unusual ________________

4 waste material ________________

5 make fun of ________________

6 worldwide ________________

2 **Now read paragraphs C and D. For each word or phrase, put a cross if there isn't a close synonym in the paragraph and write the synonym if there is.**

C

1 mad, insane ________________

2 dirty and untidy ________________

3 watchful (= paying attention) ________________

D

4 important ________________

5 business ________________

6 enthusiasm (= a feeling of energetic interest in something) ________________

7 creativity ________________

8 succeeds (= suddenly starts to be successful or popular) ________________

3 **Read the article again. For each question, choose from the people A–D. The people may be chosen more than once.**

Which person

1 has work colleagues who make fun of him/her for something he/she did? ☐

2 isn't sure they made the right choice to take their current job? ☐

3 says they are doing the perfect job for them? ☐

4 runs a business as their job? ☐

5 says they are one of a small number of people in the world doing this job? ☐

6 chose his/her job because it was unusual? ☐

7 loves the fact he/she gets to travel with his/her job? ☐

8 mentions the fact it's important to pay attention when doing their job? ☐

That's the job for me!

Have you ever wanted a job that's, well, a bit different? Check these ones out!

A Alisha

People don't believe me when I tell them what my job is. I'm a sculptor and I work with children's building blocks. It's my job to create and build models out of them! Of course, I don't spend all my time playing with toys; it's incredibly hard work. We're given themes that we have to create models for and we have quite limited budgets, but it really is my dream job. I was lucky because the company I work for only employ a few people worldwide. After I found out that the job existed, I invented a model and made a video of it and sent it to the company; that's what got me the job. I'm so glad they chose me! I think you have to go after the job that's right for you – after all, you have to do it for many years, so you might as well enjoy it.

B Dominic

Most of the time in my job, I'm hundreds of metres below the water. I'm a junior cook on a submarine, so it's not a job that you'd enjoy if you're claustrophobic! We spend long periods at sea and it can be strange not seeing daylight or being on dry land. I help to prepare three meals a day for 58 people, so it can get pretty busy. I did have one embarrassing moment, not long after I'd started. I asked what I should do with the rubbish and was told to throw it into the sea. I didn't realise we were already underwater so when I tried to open the safety hatch to go outside all the alarms went off! I should have checked first! The senior cook and other sailors still tease me about that. The best thing for me is that we get to visit lots of amazing places all over the world.

C Rob

Lots of people think I'm crazy to do my job because they think it's really dangerous. I suppose it is quite dangerous, but I don't think about that. I work in a huge aquarium and I'm responsible for cleaning out the shark tank. It can get pretty messy, especially the glass, and the public need to be able to see in! You can't take the sharks out, so I have to work surrounded by them. We get training, and the sharks have always been fed already, but still, you have to be careful. I think some of the visitors secretly hope the sharks will attack me! I could have chosen a more 'normal' job, but I would have been bored. Perhaps I'll do something else one day, but for now I'm happy.

D Lexie

You have to like chocolate to enjoy my job – and luckily I do! I started my career working as a taster for a company that produces chocolate. It sounds amazing, right? Eating chocolate all day long. The problem was that I got fed up of not being involved in making the key decisions for the company, so I started my own company two years ago. Now I run events and tastings so people can try different kinds of chocolate, and I do consultancy work for shops and clients. It's been really tough building up the business from zero, and sometimes I wonder if I should have stayed where I was. What I love most is working with people and communicating my passion for chocolate. However, I don't enjoy the paperwork side of things. I wish I didn't have to do it. I hope to employ someone to do that if the business takes off.

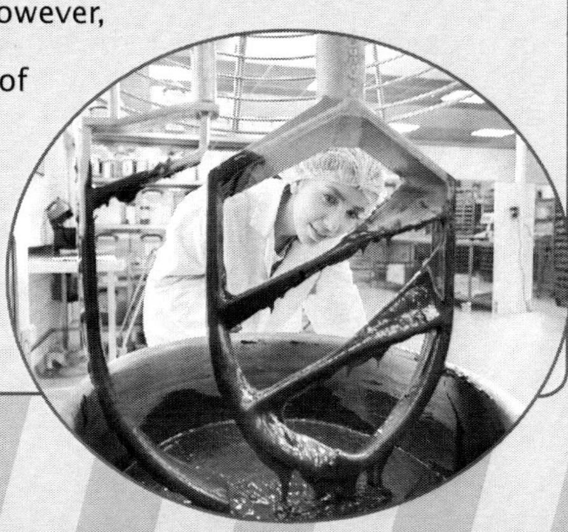

11 GRAMMAR 1 | Modals (3): modal perfect

→ Student's Book, page 116 → Grammar reference, Unit 11, Student's Book, page 159

1 **Choose the statement (a or b) that is true based on the underlined words.**

1 They ought to have informed us about the changes.
  a) They will inform us.
  b) They didn't inform us.

2 It could have been much worse; they could have sacked you.
  a) They decided not to sack you.
  b) You lost your job.

3 She may have taken the files when she left, but we have no proof.
  a) She didn't take the files.
  b) We aren't sure if she took the files.

4 It's not your fault. You couldn't have known he was listening.
  a) You knew he was listening.
  b) There was no way you could know he was listening.

5 He shouldn't have accused her of lying in front of everyone.
  a) He was wrong to accuse her of lying.
  b) He didn't accuse her of lying.

6 You needn't have sent me the email.
  a) An email wasn't sent.
  b) An email was sent.

2 **Match to make sentences.**

1 The office manager ought to ____
2 The weekly meeting should ____
3 You needn't ____
4 He may ____
5 Abby couldn't ____
6 They could ____

a) have ended by now as it started three hours ago.
b) have done that to a colleague; she's far too nice a person.
c) have ordered more supplies last week, but didn't.
d) have spoken to the manager, but I don't know for sure.
e) have interviewed more candidates, but they decided not to.
f) have ordered more paper; there's some in the cupboard.

3 **Complete the dialogue with the words in the box.**

couldn't | might | must | should | would | wouldn't

Sid: Why weren't you at the meeting?
Dom: It isn't in my diary. I (**1**) __________ have forgotten to add it in.
Sid: Well, the boss is pretty angry. She said you (**2**) __________ have been there because it concerned one of your projects.
Dom: I know, I know! I (**3**) __________ have been there if I hadn't been so busy!
Sid: That's no excuse, Dom. We're all busy and under a lot of pressure.
Dom: Is she still here? I don't want to run into her if she's in a bad mood.
Sid: She (**4**) __________ have left already, but I'm not sure.
Dom: (**5**) __________ you have called me when you realised I wasn't there? It (**6**) __________ have killed you to help out a colleague!

11 VOCABULARY | Word formation | Phrasal verbs | Topic vocabulary

→ Student's Book, page 117 → Vocabulary reference, Student's Book, page 167

1 **Complete each short text with the words in the box in the correct form.**

act | direct | manage

As a (**1**) __________, Richard is a perfectionist. Some (**2**) __________ don't like that, but others welcome the opportunity to work with him. Because he's well known and has a great reputation, most agency (**3**) __________ want their clients to appear in his films.

edit | operate | produce

Lots of people are involved in making a film. These include the (**4**) __________, whose job it is to find money to make the film, the camera (**5**) __________, who film the action, and the film (**6**) __________, who cuts unwanted scenes and fits pieces of film together to make a finished movie.

advise | news | report

The news was interesting tonight. According to a (**7**) __________ outside the Prime Minister's office, a government (**8**) __________ has been arrested. We don't know what he's been accused of yet, but the (**9**) __________ said there would be an update as soon as more information was available.

build | inspect | supervise

The new school can't open because it isn't safe. Apparently, the **(10)** __________ used very cheap materials and the **(11)** __________ in charge didn't spend enough time at the site to notice. Luckily, a building **(12)** __________ from the local council discovered the problem before classes began.

counsel | lecture | present

Did you watch *Teens In Trouble* last night? They had a **(13)** __________ on the show to give teenagers advice on avoiding bad behaviour, and a university **(14)** __________ who is an expert in child psychology. They disagreed strongly and the **(15)** __________ of the show had to stop them from attacking each other!

2 Complete the sentences with the phrasal verbs in the box.

come round | come up | get by
get through | put forward | put through
stand in for | take over

1 If I can find a second job, I'll be able to __________________ and also save for a car.
2 Klarey __________________ some great ideas, but her manager claimed them as his own!
3 If we can __________________ a few more big sites, we'll own the biggest social network site on the planet!
4 The receptionist tried to __________________ to the manager, but his line was busy.
5 Our manager will never __________________ to the idea of free lunch for employees.
6 You always seem so tired. I don't know how you __________________ the working day.
7 If any problems __________________, don't hesitate to call me on my mobile number.
8 Lucia is going to __________________ me at the office while I'm away on holiday next week.

3 Match the words and phrases in the box to the statements.

be made redundant | give someone the sack
overtime | part-time | salary | temporary
unemployed | wages

1 'Unfortunately, we have to ask you to leave. What you've done isn't acceptable here.' __________
2 'Some of the staff work extra hours in the evening and at the weekend.' __________
3 'Alice isn't full-time. She only works on Mondays, Wednesdays and Fridays.' __________
4 'The employees earn about £26,000 per year and they get paid monthly.' __________
5 'Because of the difficult economic situation, some of your jobs won't exist anymore. We're really sorry.' __________
6 'There are very few job vacancies and 20% of the young people in our city aren't working.' __________
7 'Graham earns £7.80 per hour and works four 10-hour shifts a week.' __________
8 'Your contract isn't permanent. It's for the next three months.' __________

11 GRAMMAR 2 | The causative

→ Student's Book, page 119 → Grammar reference, Unit 11, Student's Book, page 159

1 Match each pair of sentences to their meanings (a or b).

1 I had my hair done for the interview. ____
2 I had done my hair before I went to the interview. ____
a) I did it myself. **b)** Someone did it for me.
3 We have to paint the office tomorrow. ____
4 We're having the office painted tomorrow. ____
a) We'll do it. **b)** Someone else will do it.
5 You didn't need to have the alarm checked. ____
6 You needn't have checked the alarm. ____
a) You checked it. **b)** Someone checked it for you.
7 Did you get the package I sent you? ____
8 Did you get the package sent? ____
a) I sent a package. **b)** You sent a package.

2 Choose the correct words.

1 She had her assistant **the report type / type the report** and then she checked it.
2 I'll have **my lawyer prepare / prepared my lawyer** the contract as soon as possible.
3 The employees are going to **pay their bonuses / get their bonuses paid** tomorrow.
4 That's the salon where I **have my hair cut / have cut my hair** every few months.
5 He'd had his car fitted **by / with** an alarm before someone tried to steal it.
6 Drew's teeth are terrible! He's already **remove two / had two removed** this month.
7 We can't deliver anything now because **we have / we're having** the van serviced.
8 Would you have your house painted **by / with** an inexperienced decorator?

11 LISTENING | Multiple matching

→ Student's Book, page 118

1 Choose an attitude/feeling from the box to match the underlined actions/reactions.

amused | angry | disappointed | relieved surprised | tired | upset | worried

1 I was worried for a moment when the interviewer asked me a tricky question, but luckily I answered confidently and it all went well. ____________
2 My job interview is coming up next week and I'm absolutely dreading it; in fact, it's keeping me awake at night. ____________
3 I really wasn't expecting to get the job, so when they called me I was too shocked to speak. ____________
4 Unfortunately, the job didn't live up to my expectations for a number of reasons so I started looking for a new one. ____________
5 What my colleague said was really hurtful and I started to cry. ____________
6 When I got home, I could hardly keep my eyes open and so I went straight to bed. ____________
7 She didn't say a word. She just turned and stormed out of the meeting, slamming the door as she left. ____________
8 I didn't say anything at the time, but when she left the office, I started to laugh. ____________

2 20 You will hear five extracts about problems at work. Choose from A–H what each speaker says about it. There are three extra letters you do not need.

A I'm feeling very stressed at work.
B I'm reluctant to upset a colleague.
C I'm worried that my boss is planning something.
D I can't stand one of my close colleagues.
E I suspect my colleague has done something dishonest.
F I don't know how to put my plan into action.
G I've been offered two jobs and must choose one.
H I feel guilty for following my heart.

Speaker 1: ☐
Speaker 2: ☐
Speaker 3: ☐
Speaker 4: ☐
Speaker 5: ☐

11 SPEAKING | Photo task

→ Student's Book, page 120

1 21 Look at the two photos and the exam task. Then listen to the two students (David and Jess) doing the task and answer the questions D (David) or J (Jess).

Here are your photographs. They show two different places where people work. I'd like you to compare the photographs and say what you think it's like to work there.

1 Which student speaks for less than one minute? **D / J**
2 Which student speaks in a calm and contolled way? **D / J**
3 Which student introduces their ideas clearly? **D / J**
4 Which student constantly gives irrelevant personal opinions? **D / J**
5 Which student makes the most relevant comparisons between the two places? **D / J**
6 Which student doesn't properly understand the second part of the task? **D / J**

2 **Answer the exam question below.**

Compare the photographs and say **why you think the people chose these jobs**.

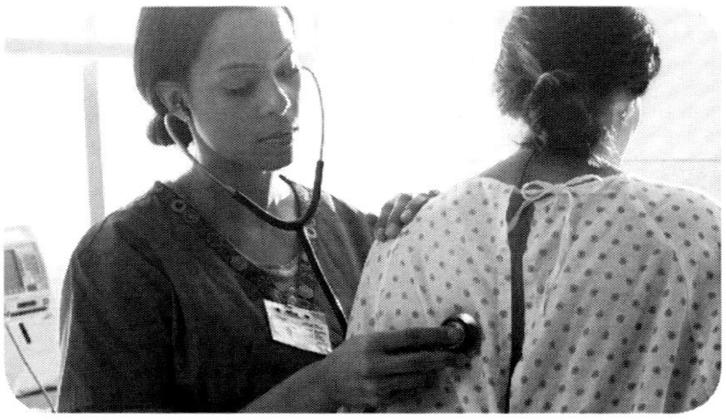

11 USE OF ENGLISH | Multiple-choice cloze

→Student's Book, page 121

1 **Complete the sentences with the words in the box. Then match sentences 1–8 to their logical responses (a–h).**

by | end | get | go | off | take | up | with

1 Why do you put up ____________ his constant lateness? ____
2 Fifty years ago, a family could get ____________ on one salary. ____
3 You really should ____________ for a career in sales. ____
4 My boss made me ____________ on too much work. ____
5 I can't ____________ through the morning without coffee. ____
6 A problem has come ____________ at the office. ____
7 Henry will ____________ up becoming the manager. ____
8 I've gone ____________ my job and no longer enjoy it. ____

a) In fact, I can't concentrate on anything until I have some.
b) It would be better to fire him and employ someone responsible.
c) The new manager is to blame – I can't stand him.
d) It seems they can't find an important file, so I've got to go there.
e) You're really good with people and you make them feel comfortable.
f) I know he just started as an assistant, but he's got a great future.
g) These days, though, not even two are enough.
h) I have to make it clear to him that I can't do it all on my own.

2 **Choose the correct words.**

1 Who's going to stand **up** / **out** / **in** for you at work while you're away?
2 We expected some problems to come **about** / **on** / **up**.
3 What will happen to our jobs if the company is taken **out** / **up** / **over**? Will we lose them?
4 No-one was able to put **forward** / **on** / **up** any ideas for the new advertising campaign.
5 Do you think the boss will come **across** / **round** / **up** to the idea of us leaving early every Friday?
6 I telephoned the company and asked to be put **through** / **out** / **in** to the manager's office.

3 **Choose the correct word for each gap.**

Work horoscopes: Aquarius – the week ahead

Get ready, Aquarius. You're going to have a busy week and you'll have to (**1**) ____________ up with added pressure. At work, you'll be asked to take (**2**) ____________ extra responsibilities and you may find yourself working (**3**) ____________ to finish everything in time. But don't worry – to your (**4**) ____________, your manager will help you. They may even employ (**5**) ____________ staff to help you for a week or two.

Although you prefer to do things yourself, you need to (**6**) ____________ round to the idea that accepting help is not a sign of weakness. Don't worry. No one wants to (**7**) ____________ you the sack.

Remember! It's going to be a tough week, but you will (**8**) ____________ through it by keeping calm.

	a)	b)	c)	d)
1	**a)** come	**b)** put	**c)** take	**d)** work
2	**a)** on	**b)** in	**c)** out	**d)** down
3	**a)** extra time	**b)** part-time	**c)** overtime	**d)** full-time
4	**a)** comfort	**b)** rescue	**c)** benefit	**d)** relief
5	**a)** redundant	**b)** permanent	**c)** temporary	**d)** shift
6	**a)** come	**b)** look	**c)** go	**d)** bring
7	**a)** get	**b)** make	**c)** do	**d)** give
8	**a)** walk	**b)** be	**c)** get	**d)** go

11 WRITING | A letter / An email

→Student's Book, pages 122–123 →Writing reference, Student's Book, page 172

1 Complete the exam skill advice with the words in the box.

chatty | people in authority | relationship | respectful | young people

1 Always think about what your ______________________ is with the person you're writing to, so you know if your style should be formal or informal.

2 Informal texts are ______________________, friendly and conversational. They are for friends, close family members or ______________________.

3 Formal texts are serious or ______________________ rather than friendly. They are for (older) ______________________ and people we don't know well.

2 Read the texts and choose the correct answers.

1 Text **A** / **B** is informal.

2 In text **A** / **B** the writer addresses the recipient using their surname.

3 Text **A** / **B** recommends a person, giving reasons.

4 Text **A** / **B** is giving advice to a friend, including an opinion.

A

To: Maria

Subject: job interview

Hi Maria,

Thanks for your email yesterday. It was great to hear from you! I'm glad your exams went OK!!

You said you had got a job interview for a part-time job and wanted some tips for it. You should definitely look on the company website and find out as much about them as you can. That way, you can explain how you would be a good candidate for them.

If I were you, I'd look at the job advert again and prepare some questions they might ask you. There are lots of websites with typical interview questions which you could look at to help you. I think you should find someone to practise with, too. What about doing a practice interview on Skype? That way you won't be so nervous in the interview!

Anyway, let me know how you get on. Good luck!

Bye for now!

Love,

Debbie

B

Dear Mrs Bolton,

I am writing with regard to your request for suggestions about people with particularly interesting skills or abilities who could appear in the school magazine. I believe I know the perfect person.

The writer Monica Ali is the author of four successful books, one of which was made into a film. In addition, she was a student at this school.

I have little doubt that readers would be fascinated to know more about her career, how her studies helped her succeed, what it is like to be a writer and the skills you need. She is a good career model for aspiring writers.

I have some information about her work and achievements. Please let me know if you would like me to give this to the magazine editor or if you would like me to write a short article.

I look forward to hearing from you.

Yours sincerely,

Sam Owen

Year 11

3 Read texts A and B again and find two or three …

1 expressions for informal letters/emails ______________________

2 expressions for formal letters/emails ______________________

PROGRESS CHECK

1 Choose the correct answers.

1 Everyone in the shop works three early and three late __________ a week.
a) wages **b)** hours **c)** shifts

2 Kim __________ in for me at work when I took my annual holiday.
a) stood **b)** came **c)** helped

3 Five people in our department were __________ redundant last week.
a) given **b)** taken **c)** made

4 I need more money than I'm currently earning in order to get __________ .
a) on **b)** by **c)** up

5 Jess is a __________-time employee. She works 35 hours a week.
a) part **b)** full **c)** normal

6 The company __________ Jed because he was always late for work.
a) bagged **b)** sacked **c)** trashed

7 I thought you wanted to be a doctor, so why did you __________ off the idea?
a) come **b)** take **c)** go

8 It took ages before I was finally put __________ to the sales department.
a) up **b)** through **c)** in

9 The company is growing and has many __________ at the moment. You can apply online.
a) vacancies **b)** contracts **c)** unemployed

10 The idea I __________ forward was great, but my manager claimed it was his!
a) pushed **b)** put **c)** brought

2 Choose the correct words.

1 You **must** / **should** have worn a suit to your interview. Why didn't you?

2 He only started writing the report an hour ago, so he **can't** / **needn't** have finished it already!

3 Honestly, I **may** / **would** have called you earlier, but I was stuck in a meeting.

4 It doesn't say who sent the package, but it **must** / **can't** have been the general manager. That's her handwriting on the address.

5 She ordered more pens, but she **needn't** / **couldn't** have because there were plenty already.

6 I'm glad you didn't shout at the boss; it **wouldn't** / **shouldn't** have been a wise thing to do.

7 The package **might** / **should** have been delivered by now; I wonder what's holding it up.

8 My computer works now. I finally **had it repaired** / **had repaired it** last week.

9 I'm getting my new CV checked **by** / **with** my sister who is an editor.

10 I wonder if I should **have** / **have had** my hair done before the presentation tomorrow.

11 Poor Holly! She **had** / **got** her mobile phone stolen at the training seminar.

12 I've been having my house **painted** / **painting** this week so I'm staying at a hotel.

Cumulative progress 1 2 3 4 5 6 7 8 9 10 11 12

3 Write one word in each gap.

Fired and rehired: the story of Steve Jobs

When Steve Jobs turned 30, the company he (1) __________ created – Apple – fired him. Why? Apple had become (2) __________ a big company that Jobs and his partner, Steve Wozniak, needed an executive to run it with them. Initially, all was well, but before long Jobs and the executive began to argue. They (3) __________ disagree constantly about their vision for the company, and this led to Jobs' removal from Apple. But in a strange twist, the company rehired him ten years later.

Jobs spoke about the experience in a speech. He said that (4) __________ Apple taken away from him was the best thing that (5) __________ have ever happened to him. Starting from zero again had freed him to enter one of the (6) __________ creative periods of his life. For example, during his absence from Apple, Jobs helped set up the Graphics Group, the computer animation company that later became Pixar, the hugely successful company responsible for films such as *Toy Story* and *Inside Out*.

Jobs returned to Apple in 1997 as CEO. Under his leadership, key products such as the iPod, iPhone, and iPad (7) __________ launched and as a company Apple took off, becoming one of the most popular technology brands in the world.

So (8) __________ you ever lose your job, don't panic. Remember that even one of the most successful businessmen of all time once lost his and things still turned out OK for him.

12 My hero!

READING | True/false with explanation

→Student's Book, pages 124–125

1 **Quickly read the first two paragraphs of the article opposite. Find and underline examples of the following things.**

1 personality adjectives for a traditional hero
2 personality adjectives for an anti-hero

2 **Write a word from the article to complete these phrases used to introduce examples.**

1 ___________ **example**, instead of being brave they might be scared; …
2 … **is a** ___________ **example of** the villain anti-hero.
3 ___________ **look at** Tony Stark (Ironman) …

3 **Decide if each statement is T (True) or F (False). Then identify the sentence in the article which supports your decision. Write the first four words of this sentence.**

1 The author of this text is a big fan of conventional heroes. **T / F**
____

2 Anti-heroes are always brave. **T / F**
____

3 The Greeks invented the phrase 'anti-hero'. **T / F**
____

4 Dracula is the most popular film character ever. **T / F**
____

5 Dracula is a good example of an anti-hero because of his human qualities. **T / F**
____

6 Today's superheroes can have anti-hero qualities. **T / F**
____

7 Anti-heroes mirror the complexity of the world we live in. **T / F**
____

4 **Find the following words and phrases in the article and match them to their meanings.**

1 stereotypes	(paragraph 2) ____	**a)** faults, weaknesses
2 bad-tempered	(paragraph 2) ____	**b)** varies, changes
3 villain	(paragraph 2) ____	**c)** love, dedication, loyalty
4 flaws	(paragraph 3) ____	**d)** typical versions of something
5 straightforward	(paragraph 4) ____	**e)** normal, typical, usual
6 wavers	(paragraph 4) ____	**f)** interesting, fascinating
7 compelling	(paragraph 5) ____	**g)** bad guy, opposite of hero
8 devotion	(paragraph 6) ____	**h)** quick to become angry

www.heroes...

The age of the anti-hero

■ **by Larry King (Chief Reporter)**

We all have a good idea of what we think a traditional hero is like – brave, selfless, and usually good-looking – at least, they are in the movies. The problem with these heroes is that they are also usually incredibly dull. So thank goodness for the anti-hero.

Anti-heroes are protagonists who do not conform to the usual hero stereotypes. For example, instead of being brave they might be scared; they might be unreliable instead of being trustworthy. They might even be insecure, ugly or bad-tempered. While traditional heroes always do the right thing, anti-heroes can be selfish and rebellious. In fact, they may not be heroic at all, but a mixture of hero and villain.

Anti-heroes are not a new idea. They appeared in the comedies and tragedies of ancient Greek theatre. However, the term itself was first used in the 17th century. What they all tend to have in common is that we can relate to them for their all too human flaws.

Count Dracula, the protagonist of Bram Stoker's novel *Dracula*, is a classic example of the villain anti-hero. His character has fascinated people since the book was first published in 1897. Over 200 films have been made about him (second only to the character of Sherlock Holmes, the most popular film protagonist ever). The fascination with Count Dracula lies in the fact that he is a complex character. He can feel love, jealousy and anger just like humans. Although he is a vampire, he is not a straightforward villain since he wavers between following the path of evil and wanting a peaceful end to his immortality.

It is this fine line between good and evil that makes many anti-heroes so compelling. You might be surprised to know that for fans of the *Harry Potter* stories, Severus Snape is one of the most popular characters. From

the very first story to the last, Snape is consistently unlikeable – a mean-spirited and bitter man, determined to make life difficult for Harry. However, in the end we finally learn who Snape really is, and what motivates him. In the light of this, we really understand what a brave and noble person he really is.

In fact, when you look at most famous heroes in literature and film, it's a similar story. Holden Caulfield, the 17-year-old narrator and protagonist in *The Catcher in the Rye*, and Captain Jack Sparrow in *Pirates of the Caribbean* are both complex characters who do terrible things, yet for one reason or another they have inspired the devotion of thousands, if not millions, of fans. Even modern superheroes seem to be based on the anti-hero idea. Just look at Tony Stark (Ironman) – not exactly the ideal role model.

Anti-heroes reflect the world we live in, a world in which issues are not always black or white, right or wrong, and people have their faults. In fact, it is their imperfections that are more interesting. Heroes who make mistakes, and sometimes do the wrong thing represent something far more fascinating than the traditional heroes of old – they represent our own journey through life and the choices we must make.

12 GRAMMAR 1 | The future (2): continuous, perfect simple and continuous

→ Student's Book, page 126 → Grammar reference, Unit 12, Student's Book, page 160

1 Match the sentences to what they describe.

1 At midday tomorrow, the volunteers will be arriving for their training. ____
2 By the time it rains, the farmers will have been waiting for months. ____
3 At the end of the week, we'll be having a meeting with the director of the charity. ____
4 The event will have finished by the time you get there. ____

a) an action completed between now and a point in the future
b) an action in progress at a point in the future
c) an action continuing up to a point in the future
d) a future event that is expected to happen

2 Choose the correct words.

1 **A:** I can't understand why Ferne is so late.
B: In a few minutes, we **will be waiting / will have been waiting** for two hours.

2 **A:** We **won't be collecting / won't have collected** money for the animal shelter this morning because of the rain.
B: That's a shame. I hope we can go out in the afternoon.

3 **A:** The others **may have left / might have been leaving** by the time you get there.
B: I hope not. I won't know where to find them.

4 **A:** Can we meet at around 3 o'clock today?
B: No, **I'll be studying / I'll have been studying** in the library then.

3 Complete the sentences with the verbs in brackets. Use the future continuous, future perfect simple or continuous tenses.

1 By November, the weather ______________________ (**become**) too cold for the homeless to sleep outdoors.
2 My father, who is a police officer, ______________________ (**not work**) tomorrow because he has the day off.
3 The firefighters ______________________ (**battle**) the forest fire for hours by the time they get it under control.
4 At 8 o'clock tomorrow, Lucy ______________________ (**serve**) breakfast to the homeless people at the shelter.
5 We ______________________ (**not finish**) preparing for the event by midday; we need more time to get ready.
6 How long ______________________ (**Bob / run**) the animal shelter when he retires later this year?
7 ______________________ (**you / drive**) to the fundraising event this evening or is someone taking you?
8 By my 18th birthday next month, I ______________________ (**help**) stray animals for three years.

12 VOCABULARY | Word formation | Collocations | Topic vocabulary

→ Student's Book, page 127 → Vocabulary reference, Student's Book, page 168

1 Complete the sentences with the words in the box in the correct form.

capital | critic | favourite | hero | ideal | race | tour | vegetarian

1 The government minister received a lot of __________ for his thoughtless comments on the current crisis.
2 Even in multicultural countries where you would expect people of all cultures to get along, __________ is sometimes a problem.
3 I tried __________ for a few months, but I stopped and went back to eating meat because I missed it.
4 The police officer was highly praised for his __________ after he saved a drowning man from certain death.
5 Millions of visitors go to Greece every summer, making __________ the biggest industry in the country.
6 Of course wealthy people are in favour of __________ – it helps them to make their money, increase it and keep it.
7 As people get older, they lose a lot of the __________ of their youth and they become less hopeful and happy.
8 Teachers must treat all of their students equally and should never show __________ in the classroom.

2 **Complete the sentences with the collocations in the box in the correct form.**

do good | do her duty | make a difference | make excuses | make (somebody) proud | make sense

The good doctor

It had always been Jenna's ambition to become a doctor. When she finally qualified, it **(1)** ______________ for her to join a medical aid charity in drought-stricken Africa. As a doctor, she believed she had a strong obligation to **(2)** ______________ and help the poor. She **(3)** ______________ her family ______________ and she also became a role model for medical students and young doctors. When she was asked what advice she would give them, she replied, 'If you know what needs to be done, do it! Don't **(4)** ______________ for the things you haven't done. Go out and **(5)** ______________ to the lives of those who are helpless. You will never regret **(6)** ______________, but you will always regret doing nothing.'

3 **Complete the dialogues with the words in the box.**

famous | infamous | kind | likeable | ordinary | polite | popular | sympathetic | typical | unknown

1 **A:** When you answer the phone, you must be __________ and thank the caller at the end of the call.
B: I will. I must say, it's very __________ of you to help me like this on my first day. I'm very grateful.

2 **A:** It's __________ of celebrities to get involved with a charity and then drop it when the next trendy cause comes along. They'll do anything for publicity and I'm sick of it.
B: Luckily, there are __________ people like us who help charities for the right reasons.

3 **A:** That young tennis player was __________ a few weeks ago; nobody had heard of him. Look at him now!
B: It's amazing, isn't it? He threw his racket at the umpire and now he's __________ . Everyone knows his name and what he did – but for negative reasons!

4 **A:** I wonder why Kenny isn't more __________ with his classmates. He hasn't got any friends at all.
B: I know, it's strange. His dad is a __________ actor, but that doesn't make people want to be his friend.

5 **A:** Have you met the new nurse in the children's ward? She's very __________ and the patients love her!
B: Yes, I've heard. She's so __________ to their problems and is willing to listen if they want to talk.

12 GRAMMAR 2 | Past tenses for the present/future

→Student's Book, page 129 →Grammar reference, Unit 12, Student's Book, page 160

1 **Match to make sentences. Use the words in italics to help you.**

1 *It's high* ____
2 *If* ____
3 *What* ____
4 *I* ____
5 *I'd* ____
6 *It's* ____

a) *rather* we chose to support a local charity that helps teenagers in trouble.
b) *time* you did something to help those less fortunate than yourself.
c) *wish* there were more volunteers here today to help us raise money.
d) *only* owners wouldn't abandon their pets when they get bored of them.
e) *about time* the council began to look after the stray animals in the city.
f) *if* you didn't have a home, a job or a future to look forward to?

2 **Choose the correct words.**

1 **I suppose** / **Suppose** you lost your job. What would you do?
2 Unless he **finds** / **found** a job, he wouldn't be able to survive financially.
3 Imagine if your house **floods** / **flooded**. What would you do?
4 I think it's time we **leave** / **left** because it's getting very late.
5 Excuse me, Mr Ritchie. **Would** / **Did** you want to speak with me?

3 **Complete the second sentence so that it has the same meaning as the first sentence, using the word given.**

1 I'd love to know who his heroes are. **WISH**
I ______________________ who his heroes are.

2 He should have won an award by now. **HIGH**
It's ______________________ an award.

3 I'd prefer us to work for the animal charity. **WORKED**
I'd ______________________ for the animal charity.

4 It's a shame I can't come to the awards ceremony. **ONLY**
If ______________________ to the awards ceremony.

12 LISTENING | Multiple choice (single extract)

→ Student's Book, page 128

1 🔈22 **Look at the first question in Exercise 2. You will hear someone saying three different sentences for the question. Decide which option (A, B or C) matches the meaning of each sentence.**

Sentence 1 ____ Sentence 2 ____ Sentence 3 ____

2 🔈23 **Listen to a radio interview with a teenager called Luke Daley. As you listen, choose the correct answer (A, B or C).**

1 Who does Luke consider to be brave?
- **A** firefighters and rescue teams who are often in danger
- **B** aid workers who dedicate their lives to helping the needy
- **C** parents who want to provide a good life for their children

2 What did Luke think he had seen at first when he was jogging?
- **A** sunlight on the water
- **B** a bird flying
- **C** a fish

3 What was Luke's first reaction to what he saw?
- **A** He stopped jogging to look at it again.
- **B** He didn't think it was important.
- **C** He knew something was wrong.

4 How did Luke feel when he went into the water?
- **A** scared
- **B** desperate
- **C** relieved

5 What do Luke and the interviewer agree on about heroes?
- **A** They show courage.
- **B** They act on instinct.
- **C** They think about others first.

12 SPEAKING | Collaborative task

→ Student's Book, page 130

1 🔈24 **Unscramble the phrases for discussing options. Then listen and check.**

1 one / we / with / Shall / this / start / ? ____________________

2 do / qualities / So / on / agree / these / we / ? / , ____________________

3 taking / about / What / risks / ? ____________________

4 should / think / we / Do / choose / you / courage / ? ____________________

5 agree / you / be / choice / confidence / that / our / second / Do / should / ?

____

6 on / if / courage / we / looks / as / It / agree / . ____________________

2 🔈25 **Read the exam task. Then listen to two students doing the task and say which two qualities they chose.**

You have about a minute to decide together which two qualities are most important in a hero.

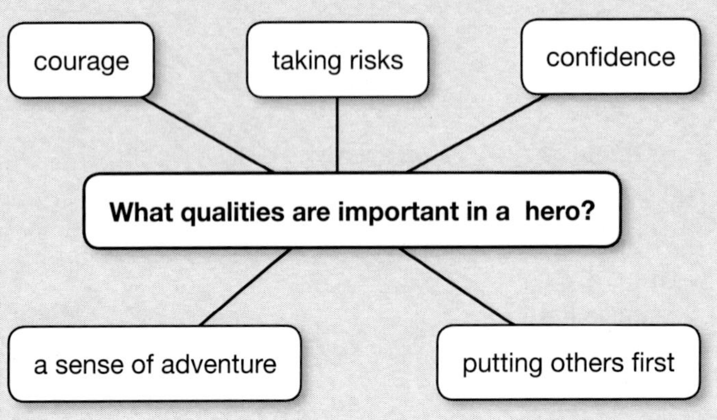

Qualities: ____________ and ____________

3 25 **Listen again and tick the things the students do during the task.**

1 Make their points clearly. ☐
2 Give their partner a chance to respond. ☐
3 Agree with each other on every option. ☐
4 Move on to a different option if they disagree. ☐
5 Reach a decision and complete the task. ☐

12 USE OF ENGLISH | Open cloze

→Student's Book, page 131

1 **Read the news report. Decide if a main verb (M) or an auxiliary verb (A) goes in each gap.**

POLICE CLASH WITH DEMONSTRATORS

Earlier today there (**1**) _____ a demonstration in the city centre. Thousands of people have (**2**) _____ gathering all morning to pressurise the government into changing the law that allows oil companies to drill near protected coastal areas. The demonstrators (**3**) _____ warned that they would (**4**) _____ arrested and fined if they continued to block traffic. The demonstrators (**5**) _____ to leave and said they were (**6**) _____ their duty as concerned citizens. The government (**7**) _____ expected to announce its decision about the law later in the year. Members of the environmental group Green Freaks say the decision should (**8**) _____ been made months ago, and that the environment minister is (**9**) _____ excuses for the oil companies.

We (**10**) _____ keep you updated on this and other stories throughout the day.

2 **Look at the report again. Think of a word for each gap. Write your answers below.**

1 __________
2 __________
3 __________
4 __________
5 __________
6 __________
7 __________
8 __________
9 __________
10 __________

3 **Write one word in each gap.**

Rosa Parks, a modern hero

It has (**1**) __________ over 60 years since an ordinary African-American woman named Rosa Parks did something quite extraordinary. It happened at a time when black people in the USA did not have the same rights as white people. Parks (**2**) __________ been travelling on a bus in Alabama, USA, when a white man ordered her to get up so that he could (**3**) __________ down. Despite rules that required black people to give their seats to white people, she refused to do so. She felt that she had a right to (**4**) __________ treated like any other passenger. As a result, she (**5**) __________ jailed and also fined $14. She didn't know it at the time, but her act of courage (**6**) __________ change American history. Her simple refusal inspired African-Americans to fight more strongly for their civil rights.

Parks showed that you don't have to be a famous leader to bring about change. Little people can (**7**) __________ a big difference. And for that, she (**8**) __________ always be remembered as a hero.

12 WRITING | An essay

→ Student's Book, pages 132–133 → Writing reference, Student's Book, page 174

1 Read the exam task and essay. Then look at the checklist. Which thing did the writer NOT do?

1 ☐ I've talked about the two notes in the question.
2 ☐ I've come up with my own idea for a third point.
3 ☐ I've expressed my personal opinion, and given reasons for it.
4 ☐ I've given examples where necessary.
5 ☐ I've written at least four main paragraphs.
6 ☐ I've used an appropriate style for an essay.

What kind of people make the best role models for young people?

Notes
Write about:

1 politicians
2 sports stars
3 .... (your own idea)

Write your **essay**.

What kind of people make the best role models for young people?

Some people believe that politicians are good role models because they are leaders. It is true that politicians such as Nelson Mandela have shown themselves to be brave and principled. They are definitely people to admire and therefore I believe they are positive role models. However, not all politicians are trustworthy. Sports stars are another popular choice as role models. Most young people enjoy sports; consequently, they admire sports stars. These stars have many positive attributes, for example they show that success can be achieved with hard work and persistence. I think they make good role models for this reason. However, I think ordinary people in our lives, like teachers or relatives, can influence us a lot. When they work hard to be the best they can, we are inspired to be kind, help others and do our best. In conclusion, while some politicians and sports stars make good role models for young people, I tend to think that amazing ordinary people in our lives make the best role models.

2 Read the essay again.

1 Mark where the essay should be divided into paragraphs.
2 Find three examples of phrases for drawing conclusions. ____________________

3 Read the exam task in Exercise 1 again and complete the plan below with your notes.

1 Do you think pop stars make good role models? Why / Why not? Provide at least one example.	
2 Do you think scientists make good role models? Why / Why not? Provide at least one example.	
3 In your opinion, what kind of people make the best role models? Why? Provide at least one example.	
4 In one or two sentences, summarise your opinion.	

PROGRESS CHECK

1 Choose the correct words and complete the gaps with the correct form of the words in brackets.

1 This world **famous** / **popular** economist is well known for his ___________ (**critic**) of what he calls the greedy ___________ (**capital**) system that has taken over our lives. In his new book he claims that such a system only **makes** / **has** sense if there are both rich and poor, and that the system is not **sensitive** / **sensible** to the needs of the poor.

2 In the 20th century, ___________ (**tour**) really took off as an industry. Cheaper air fares meant that **typical** / **ordinary** people could travel and experience other cultures. It has **caused** / **made** a big difference to the way people plan their leisure time. Holidays now require much more **caring** / **careful** planning.

3 As a boy, Alex was filled with the ___________ (**ideal**) of youth. He had dreams of saving the world and winning the Nobel Prize. Instead, he became a firefighter displaying ___________ (**hero**) on a regular basis. He says he doesn't mind being **infamous** / **unknown** and that he is happy to **do** / **work** his duty.

2 Choose the correct answers.

1 What will you ___________________ at 10 o'clock tomorrow morning?
a) have done **b)** have been doing **c)** be doing

2 I ___________________ have found a home for the stray puppy by tomorrow.
a) would **b)** should **c)** must

3 I'm afraid I won't ___________________ the report by the time you need it.
a) be finishing **b)** have finished **c)** have been finishing

4 This time next week, I ___________________ be standing in for Lucy, but it isn't definite.
a) might **b)** will **c)** can

5 In March, the charity will ___________________ stray animals for a year.
a) be protecting **b)** have protected **c)** have been protecting

6 Shelley wishes she ___________________ how to solve the problem.
a) knew **b)** knows **c)** is knowing

7 I'd rather ___________________ care of the animals here yourself.
a) take **b)** you took **c)** I took

8 Imagine someone ___________________ your car. What would you do?
a) who steals **b)** he stole **c)** stole

9 You've been watching TV all morning. It's time ___________________ to work!
a) you went **b)** for you go **c)** you go

10 I really hate the place where I work. If only I ___________________ go there.
a) don't have to **b)** didn't have to **c)** needn't

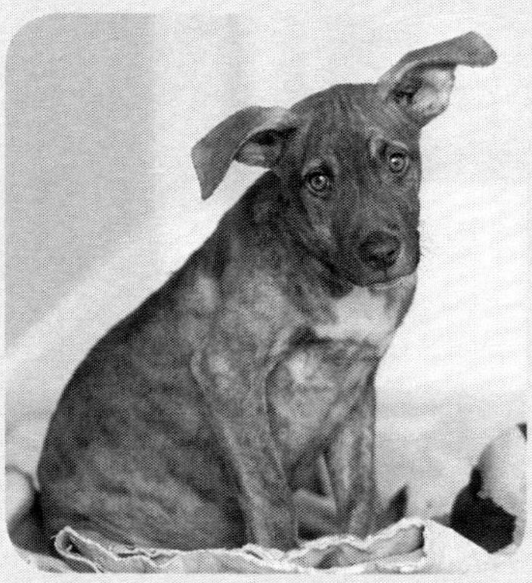

Cumulative progress 1 2 3 4 5 6 7 8 9 10 11 12

3 Write a form of the word in capitals in each gap.

Bethany Hamilton

Everyone has the potential for (**1**) ___________ . But until we are faced with a challenge – often quite a (**2**) ___________ one – we don't know what we're capable of achieving. For 13-year-old Bethany Hamilton, her dreams of becoming a professional surfer nearly ended one sunny morning in Hawaii. She was relaxing on her surfboard with her left arm moving in the water, totally (**3**) ___________ of what was beneath her. Without warning, a shark attacked her and she lost her arm. (**4**) ___________ , Bethany remained calm, and perhaps that's what saved her life. She showed amazing mental and physical (**5**) ___________ for such a young girl, and that helped her to survive the attack. In the weeks and months that followed, she (**6**) ___________ began to accept what had happened. She refused to see losing an arm as a (**7**) ___________ , and before long, she was back in the water and competing with the best women surfers in the world. This (**8**) ___________ young woman has given hope to many young people facing their own personal crises.

HERO
TERROR
AWARE
BELIEVE
STRONG
GRADUAL
ABLE
ADMIRE

Reading and Use of English • Part 1

1 hour and 15 minutes for this paper

For questions **1–8**, read the text below and decide which answer (**A**, **B**, **C** or **D**) best fits each gap.

Abele Bikila: the barefoot champion of Africa

At the Rome Olympics in 1960, an Ethiopian marathon runner named Abebe Bikila became the first black African athlete to win a gold medal. He took **(1)** .... in the marathon, replacing an injured teammate **(2)** .... the last minute.

When he **(3)** .... for the start of the race without shoes, some of the other runners laughed at him. But it didn't **(4)** .... long for Bikila to wipe the smiles off their faces. As the race progressed, they couldn't **(5)** .... with him because although he was **(6)** .... in equipment, he had plenty of determination. When he won the race in a world-record time, the press **(7)** .... crazy. He became an instant star. Not only did he **(8)** .... his own country proud, but an entire continent was grateful for its first Olympic gold medal.

1	**A**	place	**B**	part	**C**	position	**D**	post
2	**A**	at	**B**	in	**C**	for	**D**	on
3	**A**	warmed up	**B**	ended up	**C**	came up	**D**	woke up
4	**A**	have	**B**	go	**C**	take	**D**	last
5	**A**	keep up	**B**	get up	**C**	stay up	**D**	catch
6	**A**	losing	**B**	missing	**C**	lacking	**D**	needing
7	**A**	got	**B**	went	**C**	acted	**D**	had
8	**A**	show	**B**	take	**C**	help	**D**	make

Reading and Use of English • Part 2

For questions **9–16**, read the text below and think of the word which best fits each gap. Use only **one** word in each gap.

Chinatown

A common feature of some major cities around the world is 'Chinatown'. It's an area **(9)** .... the local Chinese community is based. Often quite old, with many having been established over 100 years **(10)** .... , many Chinatowns are full of history and culture.

There is no larger Chinatown outside of Asia **(11)** .... San Francisco Chinatown. It's also the oldest Chinatown in North America. On the other side of the world in Australia, Melbourne Chinatown is the longest continuous Chinese settlement in the western world. **(12)** .... thousands of miles apart, these places share a common history. **(13)** .... of them date back to the years 1840–1850. This was a time when gold **(14)** .... discovered in the USA and Australia, prompting many Chinese to leave **(15)** .... homes in China in search of wealth. They lived in neighbourhoods popular with their fellow Chinese immigrants, which came to **(16)** .... known as Chinatown. These days, Chinatown is the place to go for great Chinese cuisine and events such as New Year.

Turn over >

Reading and Use of English • Part 3

For questions **17–24**, read the text below. Use the word given in capitals at the end of some of the lines to form a word that fits in the gap **in the same line**.

Who are you?

Many people believe that our personal **(17)** .... is something that we learn **BEHAVE**
from our parents.

However, new research suggests that children's friends are extremely important in the
(18) .... of attitudes. **DEVELOP**

At first glance, this theory doesn't seem **(19)** .... After all, children spend **REASON**
more time with their friends than they do with their parents, so they will have a big
influence on how someone's **(20)** .... is shaped. Surprisingly though, the **PERSON**
experts behind this research say that while **(21)** .... with parents are important **RELATION**
because they affect the day-to-day **(22)** .... of children, they do not have **HAPPY**
long-term effects. The research also suggests that the type of home in which a child is
raised has **(23)** .... little impact on how they will grow up. **RELATIVE**

The research has proved controversial and many psychologists **(24)** .... with **AGREE**
its conclusions and reject it completely.

Reading and Use of English • Part 4

For questions **25–30**, complete the second sentence so that it has a similar meaning to the first sentence, using the word given. **Do not change the word given.** You must use between **two** and **five** words, including the word given. There are two marks for each answer.

25 Could I borrow your dictionary, please?

LENDING

Would .... your dictionary?

26 This is her first visit to a foreign country.

NEVER

She .... a foreign country before.

27 Fred didn't see the film because he was late.

IF

Fred would have seen the film .... late.

28 A group of volunteers built the new classroom.

WAS

The new classroom .... a group of volunteers.

29 It's too cold to go hiking in the mountains today.

WARM

It .... to go hiking in the mountains today.

30 Someone stole Julia's bag while she was shopping.

HAD

Julia .... while she was shopping.

Turn over >

Reading and Use of English • Part 5

You are going to read an article about the effects of modern life. For questions **31–36**, choose the answer (**A**, **B**, **C** or **D**) which you think fits best according to the text.

Dumber and Dumber?

Modern life is about progress and development. As human beings, we're supposed to improve, to become smarter with each generation. Now, while that may be true in a comparison with prehistoric people, there is an increasing amount of evidence that the humans of our era – people just like you and me – are in danger of going backwards, not forwards. The experts say that certain aspects of modern life are tiring our brains, making them slower, more stupid and less capable of original thought. What are we doing wrong? Quite a lot, actually.

Let's begin with food. There is plenty of evidence that eating the huge amounts of the fats that are found in junk food negatively affects motivation. Motivation is a key ingredient in an active brain. Not having the enthusiasm to study, read for enjoyment, go out or play sport can lead to a more sedentary lifestyle, the life of a couch potato, happy only to sit in front of a TV, watching shows that are as rubbish as the food you eat. As if that isn't bad enough, fatty diets can also damage your memory and lead to depression. Seriously, are those French fries worth it?

Another feature of modern life that affects our brains is multitasking – the ability to do many tasks at once. Multitasking shows that someone is really capable, right? Wrong. 'Multitasking' is just switching from one task to another very quickly – it doesn't mean you've done any of the tasks particularly well. In fact, studies have shown that it can be quite the opposite. Working in this way not only tires the mind, but also prevents deep and original thought because switching from task to task means you have to start from the beginning each time. In other words, it is for many a really ineffective way of getting things done and reduces the quality of the work we produce.

Constant use of information technology is another thing that affects our intelligence. 'Just Google it,' has become the answer to every question. Having unlimited information at the click of a button, wherever you are, isn't as good for you as you might think. Sure, it's great to research a school project from the comfort of your own home – no need to go to the library! But original thinking goes out the window if you can just 'take' what you need from an online source without checking your sources. You are repeating other people's ideas without questioning them and you are not thinking critically. Technically, it is also stealing, but that's another story.

Finally, let's look at the negative effects of reality TV. There are countless shows about singing contests, celebrity families, pawn shops, the rich, the poor, and everyone in between. Are they quality TV? Generally speaking, no. Do they make us dumber? Quite possibly, yes. A study by psychologists involved showing a group of volunteers a fake reality show based around the life of a football hooligan, and then asking them to take a general knowledge test. What did the results reveal? Those who had seen the reality show before the test did worse than those who had not. As they say, 'Garbage in, garbage out'.

If you think you're a candidate for stupidity, here's what you can do: put down that burger, focus on one task at a time, think with your brain not with Google, and stop watching rubbish TV. You may even like the new you.

31 What is the writer's purpose in the first paragraph?

A to describe our modern life
B to say we are going back to the past
C to make us aware of a problem
D to show that the experts are right

32 According to the writer, junk food can

A motivate people to watch TV.
B make some people very happy.
C make people less interesting.
D make you unhappy.

33 What does 'in this way' in line 38 mean?

A being busy
B doing many tasks at once
C beginning a job well
D working while you are tired

34 What do multitasking and googling have in common?

A They prevent us from concentrating.
B They affect our ability to have new ideas.
C They help us to work faster.
D They make us lazier.

35 What is the message in the paragraph about reality TV?

A Intelligence can be affected by poor quality TV.
B Although it's called 'reality TV', it's often fake.
C There are too many different reality TV shows.
D Football hooligans are stupid.

36 What does the writer NOT mention as a way to avoid stupidity?

A watch less television
B stop eating junk food
C do more voluntary work
D stop multi-tasking

Turn over >

Reading and Use of English • Part 6

You are going to read an article about a young boy who likes magic. Choose from the sentences **A–G** the one which fits each gap (**37–42**). There is one extra sentence which you do not need to use.

It's magic!

Young Henry is learning new tricks!

When I meet Henry he's wearing a red-lined cape and a black hat. He's tying knots in a rope that any experienced sailor would be proud of. **37** ______ Like magic! Which is exactly what's going on – Henry's one of ten children who are taking part in special magic camps.

All the children here have hemiplegia – a weakness or paralysis that is caused by damage to the part of the brain responsible for muscle movements. It occurs before, during or soon after birth. The paralysis is on one half of the body, on the side opposite the affected part of the brain. **38** ______

But why are they learning magic tricks? I ask 11-year-old Laura about it. Until recently, she was unable to hold things with her right hand. Then she joined the lessons and began practising the Red Ball Trick. It involves making a red ball suddenly appear and then rolling it around in the palm where it magically multiplies. **39** ______ That's because doing the trick over and over again helped to make her hand stronger.

Laura and Henry, like all children with hemiplegia, work closely with therapists to do rehabilitation exercises. However, repeating the same exercises for years can become boring. **40** ______ The magic lessons are great because they're fun to do and this helps the children to maintain their enthusiasm. The tricks are specially adapted for hemiplegic children, and they include the rehabilitation exercises that they normally do in order to be able to use both hands.

Not only is it fun but – as in Henry and Laura's cases – it's pretty effective, too. Research results show that before magic therapy, the children could only do a quarter of everyday tasks, like opening a bottle. After the camp, they could perform almost all of the tasks on their own. **41** ______

But that's not all. There are unexpected benefits, too. **42** ______ In addition, they feel less 'different' compared to their peers and more accepted. It's also pretty cool to do magic. Now, when Laura shows her classmates at school what she can do, they're impressed. 'I've never felt pride like that before,' says Laura.

A For example, if the left side of the brain is injured, then the paralysis will be on the right side of the body.

B To begin with, there's the confidence children develop when they realise they can do much more.

C As a result, it's difficult for them to stay motivated over time and they find themselves losing interest.

D While I'm still admiring his technique, there is a sudden movement and they disappear.

E Of course, I'm immediately curious about this and ask him to tell me how he does it.

F Before long, she could grasp all kinds of objects and even carry some heavy ones.

G In other words, there had been a massive improvement in their ability to function independently.

Turn over >

Reading and Use of English • Part 7

You are going to read an article about four teenagers who visited different places around the world. For questions **43–52**, choose from the teenagers (**A–D**). The teenagers may be chosen more than once.

Which teenager

was amazed by the traffic and sound levels?	**43**
had a slightly embarrassing experience?	**44**
visited a monument related to a historical personality that they admired?	**45**
talks about a building that was different from what they expected?	**46**
travelled on an unusual means of transport?	**47**
describes a building as magical and unusual?	**48**
was inspired to learn the language after the visit?	**49**
says the weather conditions were quite extreme?	**50**
says the place seemed familiar when they got there?	**51**
says the food was much better than what they usually had in their country?	**52**

Teenage travellers

Four young people talk about visiting other countries.

A Julie – Glasgow, Scotland

'We'd been studying the Romans at school for our exams, so our history teacher took us on a four-day visit to Rome. I'd never been to Italy before and I just loved it. The pasta and pizza is nothing like you get back home, it's really delicious! We walked everywhere to see all the major historical sights and the number of famous places to visit is almost overwhelming. We didn't only see monuments, though. There was time to wander around the city centre as well. I'd heard that the people are really elegant and well-dressed … and it's true! We visited the Forum and the Colosseum, but not the Vatican as it's not Roman. The best thing was the visit to Tivoli where we saw Hadrian's Villa. He's my favourite emperor and I've been learning about him at school. When we went to the Pantheon on the last day, I could almost imagine him standing in front of the enormous doors!'

B Zack – New Jersey, USA

'Last summer my parents took my sister and I to Washington D.C. because they thought it was time we saw our capital city. I actually felt as if I knew the place already because I've seen it so often in the movies and on TV. We walked up the National Mall from the Washington Monument to the Lincoln Memorial and everything looked so grand. Even though the White House was impressive, I could still imagine someone living in it, just like an ordinary house. After all the walking we were pretty tired, so we went in this weird vehicle that's a bus when it's on land, but turns into a boat when it's on water! The Potomac River is the official name for the river which passes through Washington. It's at least two million years old and the Native Americans had different names for different parts of the river. One is "Honking Geese" and we actually saw some real geese on the water swimming alongside our boat. I really enjoyed everything about the trip and I've decided that one day I want to study in Georgetown.'

C Denise – Bristol, UK

'I'm studying Russian as one of my languages, and I have a penfriend, Irina, in Moscow. So last half-term holidays I went there to visit her. It was quite chilly, but that didn't stop us going out and about to do some sightseeing. The Red Square is incredibly impressive. The cathedral, St Basil's, is like a fairy tale castle – multi-coloured and with fabulous domes. It looks as if it's made of sweets! On the other side of the square you can see parts of the Kremlin. I had always imagined it as grey and frightening, but in fact a lot of the buildings are golden and beautiful. Unfortunately, I had a bit of a disaster while I was there. I tripped and fell right in front of the entrance to Lenin's tomb. I think the soldier guarding it was trying not to laugh! After an interesting morning out, we went back to Irina's mother's flat and had borsch, a delicious, warming beetroot soup.'

D Ai Dao – California, USA

'My mother is Vietnamese and my dad is from Los Angeles. We decided to visit Hanoi, my mother's hometown. She left there when she was very young was keen to go back and visit her roots. We went in the summer so it was very humid with very high temperatures, but you get used to it. I have never seen so many motorbikes in my life! Just trying to cross the street is a real challenge, and the noise is incredible. Also, everyone, everywhere, seems to be eating all the time. They sit on tiny plastic chairs in the street, and the smell of food is wonderful. We had all my favorite dishes plus some specialities of Hanoi that I'd never tried. The best was Cha Ca La Vong, which is basically fish with peanuts, green onions and shrimp paste. We also visited many amazing temples, like Tran Quoc Pagoda, one of the oldest in Vietnam. Everyone tried to speak to me because I look just like my mom, but I don't understand Vietnamese. I really want to learn it now, though.'

Turn over >

Writing • Part 1

1 hour and 20 minutes for this paper

You **MUST** answer this question. Write your answer in **140–190** words, in an appropriate style.

1 In your English class, you have been talking about technology. Your English teacher has asked you to write an essay for homework.

Write your essay using **all** the notes and giving reasons for your point of view.

Technology is an important part of our lives. Is this a good thing or a bad thing?

Notes
Write about:

1 daily life
2 social relationships
3 .... (your own idea)

Writing • Part 2

Write an answer to **one** of the questions **2–5** in this part. Write your answer in **140–190** words, in an appropriate style. Put the question number in the box at the top of the answer sheet.

2 You have received this email from an English-speaking friend.

To: Chris
Subject: Please help

Can you help me with a class project? I have to write about a national hero from another country. Can you tell me about someone who is a national hero in your country? Tell me a little bit about who this person is and why this person should be considered as a hero for your country.

Hope to hear from you soon!

Write your **email**.

3 In your English class, you have been discussing the advantages and disadvantages of fast food.

For your homework, your teacher has asked you to write an essay outlining your opinion on the following statement.

Fast food should be banned.

Write your **essay**.

4 You have seen this announcement in an English-language website for young people.

Stories wanted

We are looking for stories for our English-language website for young people. Your story must **begin** with this sentence:

The moment Olivia opened her eyes, she knew that things had changed and her life was going to get more exciting.

Your story must include:

- a competition
- a vehicle

Write your **story**.

5 You have been asked by the editor of a school magazine to write an article on the following topic.

Technology today: it prevents students from thinking for themselves.
Is technology good or bad for education?

Write your **article**.

Turn over >

Listening • Part 1

approximately 40 minutes for this paper

26 You will hear people talking in five different situations. For questions **1–5**, choose the best answer (**A**, **B** or **C**). You will hear the recording twice.

1 You hear two young people talking about a film they saw on TV.

What do they agree about?

A the storyline

B the setting

C the excitement

2 You hear a message on a telephone answering machine.

Why is the speaker calling?

A to ask for someone's help

B to complain about something

C to persuade someone to call him

3 You overhear two colleagues talking about their boss.

How does the girl feel?

A guilty

B frustrated

C surprised

4 You hear a man talking about a new TV show.

What does he predict?

A The show will be funny.

B The show will be original.

C The show won't be popular.

5 You hear two people talking about a home remedy.

What was the girl's problem?

A a cough

B a headache

C a sore throat

Listening • Part 2

26 You will hear a young man called Andy Jones, who is a volunteer, talking about a charity called Houses for Life. For questions **6–13**, complete the sentences with a word or short phrase. You will hear the recording twice.

Andy says that many poor people lose their homes in disasters such as **(6)** .... or earthquakes.

The charity builds homes that are better and **(7)** .... so that they don't collapse.

Andy says that it takes about **(8)** .... people to build a new home in one week.

Andy explains that homes stay dry in the wet season if they are built **(9)** ....

Andy says that **(10)** .... teach the volunteers what to do.

Andy believes that being in a poor community is a good way to experience a **(11)** .... that is simpler.

Volunteers must pay for their personal expenses, but **(12)** .... , meals and transport are free.

In the last three years, Andy has been to Cambodia once and to Nepal **(13)** ....

Turn over >

Listening • Part 3

26 You will hear five short extracts in which people are talking about their hobbies. For questions **14–18**, choose from the list (**A–H**) what each speaker likes most about their hobby. Use the letters only once. There are three extra letters which you do not need to use. You will hear the recording twice.

A It teaches me new things.

B It takes my mind off things.

C It's loads of fun.

D It helps me meet like-minded people.

E I make extra money.

F I can express my creativity.

G It keeps me fit.

H It challenges me.

Speaker 1	14
Speaker 2	15
Speaker 3	16
Speaker 4	17
Speaker 5	18

Listening • Part 4

26 You will hear part of a radio interview with a young man called Grant McDonald, who makes short films. For questions **19–23**, choose the best answer (**A**, **B** or **C**). You will hear the recording twice.

19 What does Grant say about his film?

A He thinks it's too short.
B It's about a relationship.
C He put it on YouTube.

20 Why was Grant's award win unusual?

A He wasn't aware he had competed for it.
B It included an amount of money as a prize.
C It was only given to young filmmakers.

21 What career does Grant plan to follow?

A He plans to study to become a lawyer.
B He's going to give up university and make films.
C He is undecided.

22 What does Grant say about feature-length films?

A They have more characters than short films.
B They tell more stories than short films.
C He can't afford to make one.

23 What advice does Grant give to young film-makers?

A Make films without sound.
B Try to reproduce quality of feature-length films.
C Focus on filmmaking techniques rather than dialogue.

Turn over >

Speaking • Part 1

2 minutes

The examiner will ask you some questions individually.

People you know

- **Who do you most admire in your family? Tell us about him/her.**

Things you like

- **What are your favourite places in your city / home town?**
- **Do you like sports? …… (Why? / Why not?)**

Places you go to

- **Which country would you most like to visit? …… (Why?)**
- **What's the nicest place you have been to recently?**

Speaking • Part 2

4 minutes

You will do this part of the exam in pairs. Each of you will take turns to answer questions about some photographs.

Student A

Look at these photos that show people doing outdoor activities. Compare them and say **why you think people do activities like these**. Talk for about 1 minute.

Why do you think people like activities like these?

1

Student B

Which activity would you find more enjoyable? Talk for about 30 seconds.

Student B

Look at these photos that show different places. Compare them and say **why you think people go to these places**. Talk for about 1 minute.

Why do you think people go to these places?

2

Student A

Which of these places would you prefer to visit? Talk for about 30 seconds.

Turn over >

Speaking • Part 3

4 minutes

You will do this part of the exam in pairs. This task has two parts.

I'd like you to imagine your school is having a music talent contest.
Here are some ideas for what to give as a prize to the winner(s).

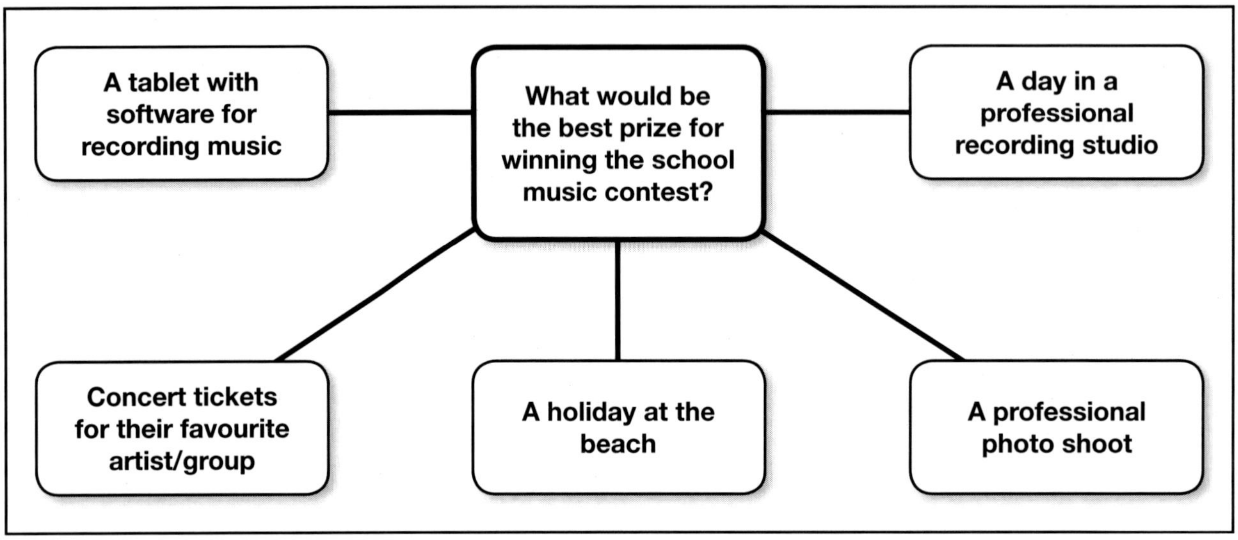

First, talk together about **why each of the options might be a good prize for the winner(s)**.
Talk for about 2 minutes.

Now you have about 1 minute to decide **which two prize options you think would be most popular**.

Speaking • Part 4

4 minutes

You will do this part of the exam in pairs. Answer the following questions together.

- **Have you ever watched any TV music talent shows? If so, what is your opinion of them?**
- **What are the benefits of learning a musical instrument?**
- **Would you like a career as a musician? ...... (Why?)**
- **How important is music in your daily life? ...... (Why?)**
- **What kinds of music are popular in your country?**
- **In what ways do you think music can be of help to some people?**

UNIT 1

Pages 4–5

READING

Exercise 1

1	E	3	A	5	F
2	C	4	D	6	B

Exercise 2

1	B	3	C	5	C
2	A	4	D		

Exercise 3

1 unplug
2 bombardment
3 tech dependence
4 attention span
5 retreat
6 eatery
7 life coach
8 clarity of mind

Page 6

GRAMMAR 1

Exercise 1

1	b	3	a	5	b
2	b	4	a	6	a

Exercise 2

1 tell
2 think
3 am joking
4 work
5 is thinking
6 see
7 feel
8 look
9 are having
10 don't think

Exercise 3

1 isn't listening
2 spends
3 are watching
4 works
5 is always borrowing
6 Are you buying
7 doesn't stream
8 is taking

Page 6

VOCABULARY

Exercise 1

1 admirable
2 reversible
3 identifiable
4 believable
5 terrible
6 accessible
7 fashionable
8 permissible
9 sensible
10 horrible
11 reasonable
12 advisable

Exercise 2

1 Take my advice
2 do me a favour
3 making progress
4 came to the decision
5 take your point
6 do my best
7 come to an agreement

Exercise 3

1 limited
2 switch
3 go
4 turn
5 upload, internet
6 fix
7 repaired
8 gadgets
9 post, online

Page 7

GRAMMAR 2

Exercise 1

1 to buy, thinking
2 to be, playing
3 to charge, doing
4 didn't use, use
5 to study, doing

Exercise 2

1	d	3	b	5	a
2	f	4	e	6	c

Page 8

LISTENING

Exercise 1

1	b	3	b	5	a
2	a	4	a		

Exercise 2

1	B	3	C	5	B
2	A	4	A		

Page 8

SPEAKING

Exercise 1

1 typical, tend
2 up, a
3 usual, time, ever, in
4 never
5 now

Exercise 2

1	c	3	a	5	d
2	b	4	e		

Exercise 3

Students' own answers

Page 9

USE OF ENGLISH

Exercise 1

1 **verb + (object) + full infinitive**
remember, tend, would like
2 **verb + (object) + *-ing***
be good at, mind, remember
3 **verb + object + bare infinitive**
make, see

Exercise 2

1	c	4	b	7	b, c
2	b	5	a, b	8	a, b
3	a, c	6	c		

Exercise 3

1 good at working out
2 agreed to share
3 mind me/my going / mind if I go
4 don't remember turning off
5 tends not to waste
6 made me drop

Page 10

WRITING

Exercise 1

1 might
2 phrases

Exercise 2

1	C	3	D
2	A	4	B

Exercise 3

1 favour
2 accept
3 totally
4 support

Exercise 4

Students' own answers

Page 11

Progress check

Exercise 1

1 do you think, to work
2 is calling, to fix
3 surfing, am doing
4 making, saves
5 going, am studying
6 say, is going

Exercise 2

1 do
2 made
3 caused, take
4 take, reasonable
5 gadgets, reversible
6 online, accessible
7 do, fix
8 permissible, switch

Cumulative progress

Exercise 3

1 B　3 A　5 A
2 B　4 D　6 B

UNIT 2

Pages 12–13

READING

Exercise 1

1 b　3 f　5 a
2 d　4 e　6 c

Exercise 2

1 an experience/event, a person talking about themselves
2 paragraphs 4 and 5
3 positive, people in general
4 more than one thing

Exercise 3

1 C　3 A　5 B
2 G　4 F　6 E

Exercise 4

1 stuff
2 contradiction
3 prioritise
4 mastering
5 accomplishing
6 boosts
7 loner
8 acquiring

Page 14

GRAMMAR 1

Exercise 1

1 saw
2 was always
3 was shining
4 were talking, were playing
5 did do
6 were you going
7 investigated
8 wasn't thinking
9 always went
10 went

Exercise 2

1 was lying
2 was bothering
3 knew
4 was looking forward to
5 didn't like
6 found
7 preferred
8 was wondering
9 spoke
10 fell
11 woke up
12 was laughing
13 replied
14 was snowing

Page 14

VOCABULARY

Exercise 1

1 d　4 i　7 c
2 a　5 b　8 f
3 h　6 e　9 g

Exercise 2

1 actively, creative
2 effectively, stressful
3 painful, thankfully
4 attractive, useful
5 productively, harmful
6 secretive, playful

Exercise 3

1 go about
2 end up
3 put up with
4 build up
5 get on with
6 carry out
7 do without
8 get up to

Page 15

GRAMMAR 2

Exercise 1

1 b　3 b　5 b
2 a　4 a

Exercise 2

1 use
2 used
3 wouldn't
4 Are
5 were used to
6 didn't use to

Page 16

LISTENING

Exercise 1

1 c　3 b
2 d　4 a

Exercise 2

1 the Amazon (rainforest)
2 explorers
3 canoe
4 five days

Exercise 3

1 experiences
2 basic
3 60/sixty % / per cent
4 warm and sticky
5 mosquitoes
6 bright blue
7 poisonous snake
8 side to side

Page 16

SPEAKING

Exercise 1

Students should tick:
1, 5, 6, 8
Students should cross:
2, 3, 4, 7

Exercise 2

1 similarity
2 both
3 while
4 Similarly
5 whereas
6 differ
7 difference
8 far
9 as
10 as

Exercise 3

Students' own answers

Page 17

USE OF ENGLISH

Exercise 1

1 e	3 a	5 b
2 c	4 d	

Exercise 2

1 d	3 e	5 c
2 a	4 b	

Exercise 3

1 get
2 nobody/no-one
3 Did
4 up
5 can/could/should

Exercise 4

1 has
2 used
3 was
4 would
5 no
6 with
7 did
8 to

Page 18

WRITING

Exercise 1

1 T	3 F	5 T
2 T	4 F	6 T

Exercise 2

Students should tick:
2, 3, 5, 6

Exercise 3

Students' own answers

Exercise 4

Students' own answers

Page 19

Progress check

Exercise 1

1 wanted
2 used to think
3 would
4 was doing
5 entered
6 realised
7 was going on
8 started
9 wasn't used to
10 felt

Exercise 2

1 lose
2 carry
3 failed
4 ended
5 succeeded
6 get
7 beat
8 put

Cumulative progress

Exercise 3

1 terrible
2 identifiable
3 effectively
4 thankfully
5 stressful
6 reversible
7 productive
8 creative

UNIT 3

Pages 20–21

READING

Exercise 1

1 the number of years of the HND diploma
2 the number of months Jamie has been a production assistant
3 the number of years Katie has worked
4 the most Marina earns per day
5 the year Stefan started working as a screenwriter
6 Jamie's salary
7 the budget for costumes on the last film Katie worked on
8 the amount of money Michael Arndt got for a screenplay

Exercise 2

1 C	4 A	7 D
2 D	5 B	8 A
3 C	6 A	

Exercise 3

1 glamorous
2 set
3 under pressure
4 artistic ability
5 rate
6 field
7 budget
8 tough

Page 22

GRAMMAR 1

Exercise 1

1 f	4 g	7 a
2 c	5 b	8 h
3 d	6 e	

Exercise 2

1 don't have to, can
2 Were you able to, should
3 ought to, Could
4 Would, can't
5 must, Do I have to
6 could, Will

Exercise 3

1 must
2 can
3 had to
4 aren't able to
5 might
6 should
7 shouldn't
8 would
9 don't have to

Page 22

VOCABULARY

Exercise 1

1 originality
2 awareness
3 popularity
4 cleverness
5 youthfulness
6 activity
7 happiness
8 weakness
9 complexity
10 openness
11 creativity
12 simplicity

Exercise 2

1 do you good, take a break
2 make fun of, take part in
3 told a joke, find it funny
4 have friends round, go online

Exercise 3

1 soap opera
2 documentaries
3 cookery show
4 sitcom
5 weather forecast
6 Chat shows
7 talent shows
8 the news

Page 23

GRAMMAR 2

Exercise 1

1 b 2 c 3 a

Exercise 2

1 c 3 a 5 c
2 b 4 b 6 a

Page 24

LISTENING

Exercise 1

1 A, C
2 B, D, E

Exercise 2

1 f 3 e 5 c
2 b 4 a 6 d

Exercise 3

1 E 3 B 5 C
2 G 4 H

Page 24

SPEAKING

Exercise 1

Students should tick:
2, 4, 5, 7, 8

Exercise 2

1 b 3 a 5 a
2 c 4 c

Exercise 3

1 d 3 c 5 b
2 e 4 a

Page 25

USE OF ENGLISH

Exercise 1

1 a 3 c 5 c
2 c 4 b

Exercise 2

1 belief
2 loss
3 capability
4 thinkers
5 choice
6 decision
7 weakness
8 popularity

Page 26

WRITING

Exercise 1

1 imagine
2 adjectives
3 reasons, explain, example

Exercise 2

1 B 3 A
2 D 4 C

Exercise 3

1 realistic
2 thought-provoking
3 ordinary
4 convincing

Exercise 4

Students' own answers

Page 27

Progress check

Exercise 1

1 can't
2 had to
3 shouldn't
4 Will (you) be able to
5 must
6 is allowed to
7 could
8 ought to

Exercise 2

1 take
2 music
3 tells
4 wildlife
5 do
6 game
7 found
8 forecast
9 take
10 reality shows
11 making
12 documentary
13 have
14 cookery
15 go
16 soap operas

Cumulative progress

Exercise 3

1 B 4 C 7 B
2 D 5 D 8 C
3 C 6 A

UNIT 4

Pages 28–29

READING

Exercise 1

1 F 3 T
2 T 4 F

Exercise 2

1 New York Transit Museum
2 Times Square
3 the NYC pizza tour
4 Since the 1920s
5 Canal Street (shops)
6 New York Transit Museum
7 Century 21 department store

Exercise 3

1 hunt
2 cuisine
3 pose
4 trendiest
5 auditioning
6 cut-rate
7 authentic
8 pushy

Page 30

GRAMMAR 1

Exercise 1

1 been waiting
2 looked
3 been gardening
4 visited
5 found
6 been building
7 thought
8 been learning

Exercise 2

1 have been trying, haven't had, has gone
2 has been going, has had, hasn't become
3 hasn't been painting, has already finished, has just run out of
4 Have you seen, haven't wished, have been looking

Exercise 3

1 ever
2 just
3 yet
4 once
5 already
6 never
7 Up
8 since
9 for

Page 30

VOCABULARY

Exercise 1

1 suburbs
2 block of flats
3 services
4 centre
5 parking space
6 office block
7 car park
8 subway
9 attractions
10 store
11 Tube
12 city centre

Exercise 2

1 regardless, have no intention
2 covered with, dispose
3 fed up, find a solution

Exercise 3

1 unaware
2 disability
3 disappeared
4 uncomfortable
5 inability
6 disadvantage
7 unbelievable
8 unable
9 disagree
10 insecure

Page 31

GRAMMAR 2

Exercise 1

1 doesn't she
2 haven't you
3 is it
4 does it
5 shall we
6 don't they
7 won't he
8 do they

Exercise 2

1 Which city did Bruce like the best on his trip?
2 Who took these beautiful photos of Amsterdam?
3 Where in New York do your cousins live?
4 What happened when you lost your passport?
5 Why did you cancel your trip to Barcelona?
6 How come you decided to study in Tokyo?
7 What about walking to the museum?
8 How do you know which bus to take?

Page 32

LISTENING

Exercise 1

1 a 2 b 3 a
4 b 5 a 6 b 7 a 8 b

Exercise 2

1 C 2 B 3 A 4 C 5 B

Page 32

SPEAKING

Exercise 1

1 true
2 forget
3 opposite
4 point
5 agree
6 a point
7 in that
8 extent

Phrases for agreeing (A)
That's true. That's a good point. That's right up to a point. There's something in that. I agree to a certain extent.

Phrases for disagreeing (D)
Let's not forget … I think the opposite. I don't entirely agree.

Exercise 2

Students' own answers

Page 33

USE OF ENGLISH

Exercise 1

1 take, centre
2 centre, stores
3 access, services
4 tower, dispose
5 intention, space

Exercise 2

1 c 2 a 3 d 4 b 5 a 6 c 7 d 8 b

Page 34

WRITING

Exercise 1

1 easier, more convincing
2 have to, can

Exercise 2

1 F 2 F 3 T

Exercise 3

1 as
2 instance/example
3 example
4 like

Exercise 4

1	A	3	D	5	D
2	D	4	A	6	D

Students' own answers

Page 35

Progress check

Exercise 1

1 capital
2 intention
3 block of flats
4 parking spaces
5 virtual
6 solution
7 attractions
8 suburbs

Exercise 2

1	c	4	b	7	c
2	b	5	a	8	a
3	a	6	c		

Cumulative progress

Exercise 3

1 is
2 been
3 since
4 will
5 have
6 used
7 was
8 shall

UNIT 5

Pages 36–37

READING

Exercise 1

1	e	3	f	5	d
2	a	4	b, g	6	c

Exercise 2

1	D	3	A	5	D
2	C	4	B		

Exercise 3

1 determined
2 phenomena
3 marks
4 lunar
5 phases
6 rituals
7 common practice
8 mythology

Page 38

GRAMMAR 1

Exercise 1

1	b	5	b	9	a
2	b	6	a	10	b
3	a	7	b	11	b
4	a	8	a	12	b

Exercise 2

1 will get
2 are getting
3 are going to get
4 get

Exercise 3

1 are having, shall
2 'm going to buy, won't be
3 rains, might
4 is going to hit, will catch
5 are we going to make, 'll use
6 'm not going, will lend

Page 39

VOCABULARY

Exercise 1

1 decorate, stimulates
2 motivate, equate
3 desperate, fortunate
4 activate, evaluate
5 considerate, affectionate

Exercise 2

1 down
2 out
3 back on
4 off
5 for
6 up to
7 down
8 off

Exercise 3

1 board games
2 yoga
3 painting
4 blogging
5 online gaming
6 social networking
7 mountain biking
8 DJing
9 scuba diving
10 photography
11 martial arts
12 programming

Page 39

GRAMMAR 2

Exercise 1

1 much fun as
2 the most exciting
3 much
4 more dangerous
5 the more relaxed, easier

Exercise 2

1 as good
2 better than
3 The most popular
4 earlier
5 fewer
6 the most beautiful

Page 40

LISTENING

Exercise 1

1 eye
2 extent
3 wavelength
4 principle
5 point

Exercise 2

Agreement:
be on the same wavelength

Partial agreement:
agree to a certain extent
agree in principle
be true up to a point

Disagreement:
not see eye to eye

Exercise 3

1	C	3	C	5	A
2	A	4	B		

Page 40

SPEAKING

Exercise 1

1 go to
2 get
3 becoming
4 get
5 have
6 travel

Exercise 2

1 weekend, specific, hoping
2 future, sure
3 planning, ambition, day
4 forward, point

Exercise 3

Students' own answers

Page 41

USE OF ENGLISH

Exercise 1

1 outside, at
2 up, in
3 in, after
4 on, out
5 In, in
6 out, to
7 in, of
8 off, with
9 between, across
10 down, to

Exercise 2

1 up
2 of
3 on
4 since
5 at
6 of
7 until
8 at

Page 42

WRITING

Exercise 1

1 reasons
2 for, because

Exercise 2

Giving reasons:
That's because … (paragraph 1)
because … (paragraph 2)
The reason for this is that … (paragraph 3)
Contractions:
it's … (paragraph 1)
That's … (paragraph 1)
they're … (paragraph 1)
it's … (paragraph 2)
Don't! (paragraph 2)
you'll … (paragraph 2)

Exercise 3

1 reason
2 because
3 because, about
4 suggest
5 thing

Exercise 4

Students' own answers

Page 43

Progress check

Exercise 1

1 affectionate
2 gets me down
3 despair
4 board games
5 dropped off
6 equate
7 blogging
8 sort it out
9 fortune
10 feel up to
11 stimulate
12 evaluate

Exercise 2

1 c	5 c	9 c
2 a	6 b	10 a
3 b	7 a	
4 a	8 b	

Cumulative progress

Exercise 3

1 C	4 C	7 D
2 D	5 A	8 C
3 C	6 A	

UNIT 6

Pages 44–45

READING

Exercise 1

1 a small amount
2 reduce
3 falling over
4 worried, ate

Exercise 2

1 happy
2 started
3 exact
4 at war
5 mixed with
6 put outside

Exercise 3

1 B	3 C	5 A
2 D	4 B	

Page 46

GRAMMAR 1

Exercise 1

1 c	3 e	5 d
2 a	4 b	

Exercise 2

1 drank
2 get
3 stays
4 will
5 eat
6 have
7 could
8 don't

Exercise 3

1 would
2 case
3 took
4 Unless
5 long
6 not

Page 46

VOCABULARY

Exercise 1

1 to
2 of
3 of
4 to
5 on
6 for
7 to
8 against

Exercise 2

1 relatively
2 surprisingly
3 Basically
4 early

5 regularly
6 daily
7 remarkably
8 Traditionally
9 frequently
10 hopefully

Exercise 3

1 sore throat, temperature
2 bruise, sprained
3 fever, virus
4 cold
5 cut, burn
6 allergy
7 cramp

Page 47

GRAMMAR 2

Exercise 1

1 which
2 when
3 which
4 why
5 who
6 where
7 whose
8 which

Exercise 2

1 who/that
2 which
3 whose
4 which
5 whom
6 why
7 which/that
8 who/which/that

Page 48

LISTENING

Exercise 1

1 happy
2 worried
3 surprised
4 angry

Exercise 2

1 a common
2 doesn't actually believe
3 in favour of

Exercise 3

1	B	4	C
2	C	5	B
3	A		

Page 48

SPEAKING

Exercise 1

1 prefer not
2 over
3 rather
4 for
5 for

Exercise 2

1 The reason for me
2 because
3 due to the fact
4 so
5 because of

Exercise 3

Students' own answers

Page 49

USE OF ENGLISH

Exercise 1

1	ADV	5	ADJ	9	ADJ
2	ADJ	6	ADJ	10	ADJ
3	ADV	7	ADV		
4	ADJ	8	ADV		

Exercise 2

1 easy
2 surprisingly
3 regularly
4 basically
5 extraordinary
6 strength
7 remarkably
8 freely

Page 50

WRITING

Exercise 1

Students should tick:
1, 2, 4, 5

Exercise 2

Students should mark the paragraphs to start at these points:
One of the best ways of …
Eating well is also …
Finally, rest and relaxation …

Exercise 3

Paragraph 2: a, d
Paragraph 3: c, f
Paragraph 4: b, e

Exercise 4

Students' own answers

Page 51

Progress check

Exercise 1

1 unhappy
2 of
3 for
4 true
5 comfortable
6 Hopefully
7 well
8 against
9 on
10 of

Exercise 2

1	b	5	c	9	c
2	c	6	a	10	b
3	b	7	b	11	a
4	a	8	a	12	c

Cumulative progress

Exercise 3

1	D	4	C	7	C
2	B	5	B	8	A
3	A	6	D		

UNIT 7

Pages 52–53

READING

Exercise 1

Apart from that **CO**
As a consequence **R/C**
As a result **R/C**
Before long **H**
In other words **Cl**
On the other hand **CO**
That is to say **Cl**
To begin with **H**

Exercise 2

1 explains the consequence of
2 when, becoming public
3 clarify
4 logically

Exercise 3

1	D	3	C	5	F
2	A	4	G	6	B

Exercise 4

Possible answers:
1 be sure you will do something
2 destroyed
3 do something badly
4 stopped feeling resentment or anger about something the other person had done
5 the way someone acts
6 giving someone opinions/advice/criticism about something they have done
7 in danger
8 did harm to somebody who trusted you

Page 54

GRAMMAR 1

Exercise 1

1 a 3 b 5 a
2 a 4 b

Exercise 2

1 had kept
2 had been waiting
3 hadn't heard
4 had been cleaning
5 Had the film already started
6 had ever had
7 hadn't eaten
8 hadn't been dancing
9 had just left
10 hadn't seen

Exercise 3

1 had been looking forward to
2 had just got to
3 had been
4 had spent
5 had been talking
6 had forgotten
7 hadn't taken
8 had had

Page 55

VOCABULARY

Exercise 1

1 admire
2 confide in
3 forgive
4 gossip
5 appreciate
6 support

Exercise 2

1 assistance
2 encouragement
3 development
4 relationships
5 friendships
6 membership
7 partnership
8 preference

Exercise 3

1 take after
2 drop in on
3 ripped … up
4 look up to
5 get along with
6 keeps on
7 running after
8 going round to

Page 55

GRAMMAR 2

Exercise 1

1 Even though
2 in spite of
3 despite
4 however
5 although
6 In spite of
7 Despite

Exercise 2

1 spite
2 However
3 Even
4 despite
5 Although

Page 56

LISTENING

Exercise 1

1 b 3 b
2 a 4 a

Exercise 2

1 G 3 B 5 C
2 E 4 H

Page 56

SPEAKING

Exercise 1

1 c 4 c 7 c
2 b 5 b 8 a
3 a 6 a

Exercise 2

1 c 3 d 5 b
2 e 4 a

Page 57

USE OF ENGLISH

Exercise 1

1 c 3 b 5 b
2 a 4 c 6 a

Exercise 2

1 look up to
2 in spite of her
3 had already left
4 had known her for
5 get on (very) well
6 despite not being
7 count on James
8 lost touch with each other

Page 58

WRITING

Exercise 1

1 descriptions
2 variety, continuous
3 Direct speech

Exercise 2

Possible answers:
1 Have (you) got
2 knew
3 was trying (them) on
4 've been
5 'd moved
6 hadn't been looking forward to

Exercise 3

Students' own answers

Page 59

Progress check

Exercise 1

1 to, with
2 on
3 with
4 after, up
5 on
6 in
7 after, up

Exercise 2

1 had never been
2 had been preparing
3 hadn't heard
4 Had you been dancing
5 had already left
6 Even though
7 Although
8 in spite of
9 However
10 Despite

Cumulative progress

Exercise 3

1 friendship
2 extraordinarily
3 relationship
4 assistance
5 development
6 existence
7 desperate
8 performance

UNIT 8

Pages 60–61

READING

Exercise 1

1 had very little chance of finding
2 People don't usually survive this kind of incident.
3 It was an extremely difficult journey.
4 haven't changed his lifestyle
5 an avalanche had started

Exercise 2

1	C	4	D	7	B
2	D	5	A	8	D
3	B	6	C		

Exercise 3

1	a	4	a	7	a
2	a	5	b	8	a
3	b	6	b		

Page 62

GRAMMAR 1

Exercise 1

1 as
2 with
3 of
4 in/with

Exercise 2

1 is being prepared now
2 used to be taken to the mountains
3 had been stolen from the base camp
4 old ropes shouldn't be used
5 were being carried up the mountain by
6 the climber been found
7 being told what to do by

Exercise 3

1 are covered
2 is estimated
3 has been climbed
4 shouldn't be attempted
5 is known
6 were thrown
7 had to be handed out
8 could be conquered

Page 62

VOCABULARY

Exercise 1

1 stream
2 coast, cliffs
3 slopes, mountain range
4 path, summit
5 waterfall
6 valley
7 volcano

Exercise 2

1 variation, conclusion
2 arrival, departure
3 behaviour, description
4 solution, choice
5 variety, decision

Exercise 3

1 in
2 with
3 from
4 about
5 into
6 of
7 in
8 about

Page 63

GRAMMAR 2

Exercise 1

1 is
2 wasn't
3 these
4 has
5 were
6 is
7 doesn't
8 were

Exercise 2

1 much, –
2 The, –
3 few, a
4 an, –
5 little, the
6 many, a
7 a, the
8 few/lot, the

Page 64

LISTENING

Exercise 1

1 tend
2 makes
3 seems
4 mind
5 Personally
6 view
7 if
8 disagree

Exercise 2

1 opinion
2 fact
3 fact
4 opinion
5 fact
6 opinion

Exercise 3

1 (fairly) common
2 civilisations
3 places
4 the gods
5 an ape
6 (so) amazing
7 in a war
8 ten hills

Page 64

SPEAKING

Exercise 1

1 d
2 a
3 b
4 c

Exercise 2

1 agree
2 opinion
3 far
4 opinion
5 sense
6 ask
7 Personally

Exercise 3

Students' own answers

Page 65

USE OF ENGLISH

Exercise 1

1 ADJ
2 N
3 N
4 V
5 N
6 V
7 N
8 N
9 ADJ
10 ADJ

Exercise 2

1 long
2 warmth
3 immaturity
4 grow
5 perfection
6 die
7 strength
8 possibility
9 young
10 deep

Exercise 3

1 departure
2 arrival
3 variety
4 death
5 strength
6 responsibility
7 youth
8 impossibility

Page 66

WRITING

Exercise 1

Students should tick:
1, 2, 3, 4, 5

Exercise 2

1 Hi/Hello
2 Thanks, hear
3 helps
4 Let
5 Write / See you
6 of

Exercise 3

Students' own answers

Exercise 4

Students' own answers

Page 67

Progress check

Exercise 1

1 in, summit
2 of, mountain
3 waterfall, into
4 of, volcano
5 in, coast
6 with, slope
7 from, cliff
8 about, path

Exercise 2

1 b
2 a
3 c
4 b
5 c
6 a
7 b
8 b

Cumulative progress

Exercise 3

1 be
2 who
3 The
4 by
5 had
6 or
7 piece
8 even

UNIT 9

Pages 68–69

READING

Exercise 1

a 3
b 7
c 1
d 4
e 2
f 6
g 5

Exercise 2

1 F
2 D
3 A
4 G
5 C
6 B

Exercise 3

1 pursue
2 prestigious
3 depended on
4 budding
5 go to his head
6 impressed
7 slept rough
8 spotted

Page 70

GRAMMAR 1

Exercise 1

1 told
2 stages there would be
3 denied taking my
4 whether I had learnt
5 advised me to practise
6 before

Exercise 2

1 warned me not
2 promised to help
3 suggested (that) I
4 refused to sing
5 claimed to know

Exercise 3

1 had
2 said/replied/explained
3 whether/if
4 his
5 told
6 been
7 following
8 had had
9 could
10 would

Page 71

VOCABULARY

Exercise 1

a trumpet
b tune
c drum
d music
e fiddle
f song
g ear
h bell

Exercise 2

1 a	4 h	7 f
2 e	5 c	8 g
3 d	6 b	

Exercise 3

1 b	4 c	7 d
2 e	5 g	8 f
3 h	6 a	

Exercise 4

1 violinist, perfectionist
2 journalist, accountants
3 optimist, applicant
4 contestants, assistant
5 guitarist, servants
6 specialist, attendant

Page 71

GRAMMAR 2

Exercise 1

1 b	3 a
2 c	4 c

Exercise 2

1 Do you know which band performs first?
2 I wonder if you could tell me who produced your album.
3 Could you tell me whether you like touring?
4 I'd like you to tell us who designs your costumes.
5 I'd be grateful if you could tell us when you practise.

Page 72

LISTENING

Exercise 1

A

Exercise 2

1 A
2 B, everyone wanted to be in a band
3 B, too much irrelevant information

Exercise 3

1 once
2 drummer
3 so good
4 supermarket trolley
5 Hot Jam Donuts
6 the bass
7 young and clueless
8 terrible

Page 72

SPEAKING

Exercise 1

1 might
2 could be
3 Maybe
4 Perhaps
5 to tell
6 totally, possibility
7 sure, imagine

Exercise 2

Students' own answers

Exercise 3

Students' own answers

Page 73

USE OF ENGLISH

Exercise 1

1 c	4 b	7 c
2 c	5 a	8 a
3 a	6 b	

Exercise 2

1 c	4 a	7 c
2 a	5 d	8 b
3 b	6 d	

Page 74

WRITING

Exercise 1

1 b	2 c	3 a

Exercise 2

1 T	3 T	5 T
2 F	4 T	6 F

Exercise 3

Students' own answers

Page 75

Progress check

Exercise 1

1 specialist, make
2 journalist, ring
3 drum, assistant
4 contestant, give
5 go, optimist
6 drop, violinist
7 guitarist, blow
8 go, pianist

Exercise 2

1 told
2 she enjoyed
3 that
4 to say
5 two days before
6 could tell
7 your next concert is
8 I can buy
9 I'd
10 you left

Cumulative progress

Exercise 3

1 remarkably
2 popularity
3 attractive
4 consultants
5 friendships
6 regularly
7 insecure
8 unable

UNIT 10

Pages 76–77

READING

Exercise 1

1 runners, initial
2 sections, exhausting
3 huge boulders, challenging
4 clothes
5 every 10–15 minutes, stop, enjoy

Exercise 2

1 292 runners
2 They contain 5,164 steps.
3 They get very hot.
4 absorb moisture
5 the scenery

Exercise 3

1 breathtaking
2 steadily
3 toughest
4 steep
5 sweat
6 tackle
7 dehydrated
8 strenuous

Page 78

GRAMMAR 1

Exercise 1

1 b
2 c
3 a
4 a
5 b
6 b
7 c
8 a

Exercise 2

1 such late so late
2 water enough enough water
3 too many so many
4 money enough enough money
5 so much too much

Exercise 3

1 too
2 to
3 such
4 that
5 so
6 enough
7 for
8 too
9 such
10 that

Page 78

VOCABULARY

Exercise 1

1 medics
2 leader
3 participants
4 supporter
5 coach
6 winner
7 sponsor

Hidden word: captain

			M	E	D	I	C	S			
					L	E	A	D	E	R	
P	A	R	T	I	C	I	P	A	N	T	S
	S	U	P	P	O	R	T	E	R		
					C	O	A	C	H		
						W	I	N	N	E	R
				S	P	O	N	S	O	R	

Exercise 2

1 enlarge
2 lengthen
3 strength
4 depth
5 wide
6 height
7 lower

Exercise 3

1 run off my feet
2 running around in circles
3 run the risk
4 hit the ground running
5 run a mile
6 trying to run
7 up and running
8 running start

Page 79

GRAMMAR 2

Exercise 1

1 hadn't taken
2 might not have become
3 wouldn't have won
4 hadn't been
5 hadn't gone
6 wouldn't have met
7 might not have done
8 had had
9 might have won
10 had run

Exercise 2

1 hadn't loved running, they wouldn't have joined the sports club.
2 I hadn't forgotten my sports clothes, I could have taken part in the race.
3 not have won the race if I hadn't spent three hours training every day.
4 Lucy hadn't forgotten to give me the entry form, I would have known about the fun run.

Page 80

LISTENING

Exercise 1

1 the fastest
2 world record
3 the gold medal

Exercise 2

C

Exercise 3

1 C
2 B
3 C
4 A
5 B

Page 80

SPEAKING

Exercise 1

a sadly, though
b funny
c honest, sounds
d counts
e actually

Exercise 2

1 d
2 b
3 e
4 c
5 a

Exercise 3

Students' own answers

Page 81

USE OF ENGLISH

Exercise 1

1 trained
2 run
3 go
4 would have won
5 will be
6 had rained
7 would enjoy
8 do

Exercise 2

zero conditional: 2, 8
first conditional: 3, 5
second conditional: 1, 7
third conditional: 4, 6

Exercise 3

Questions 4 and 5

Exercise 4

1 such a cold day
2 is the length of
3 was not big enough
4 you run the risk of
5 Sara hadn't broken
6 are too high for people

Page 82

WRITING

Exercise 1

1 c
2 a
3 b

Exercise 2

1 F
2 F
3 F
4 T
5 F
6 T

Exercise 3

Students should tick:
5, 7

Exercise 4

Students' own answers

Page 83

Progress check

Exercise 1

1 medics
2 mile
3 widen
4 ground
5 supporters
6 deep
7 feet
8 fundraiser

Exercise 2

1 were so many people
2 we might have won
3 not strong enough to finish
4 was such an exciting event
5 I had felt well/better
6 too many people applied

Cumulative progress

Exercise 3

1 C
2 A
3 B
4 B
5 C
6 C
7 D
8 B

UNIT 11

Pages 84–85

READING

Exercise 1

1 worldwide
2 glad
3 strange
4 rubbish
5 tease
6 all over the world

Exercise 2

1 crazy
2 messy
3 careful
4 key
5 company
6 passion
7 X
8 takes off

Exercise 3

1 B
2 D
3 A
4 D
5 A
6 C
7 B
8 C

Page 86

GRAMMAR 1

Exercise 1

1 b
2 a
3 b
4 b
5 a
6 b

Exercise 2

1 c
2 a
3 f
4 d
5 b
6 e

Exercise 3

1 must
2 should
3 would
4 might
5 Couldn't
6 wouldn't

Page 86

VOCABULARY

Exercise 1

1 director
2 actors
3 managers
4 producer
5 operators
6 editor
7 reporter
8 adviser
9 newsreader
10 builder(s)
11 supervisor
12 inspector
13 counsellor
14 lecturer
15 presenter

Exercise 2

1 get by
2 put forward
3 take over
4 put me through
5 come round
6 get through
7 come up
8 stand in for

Exercise 3

1 give someone the sack
2 overtime
3 part-time
4 salary
5 be made redundant
6 unemployed
7 wages
8 temporary

Page 87

GRAMMAR 2

Exercise 1

1 b
2 a
3 a
4 b
5 b
6 a
7 a
8 b

Exercise 2

1 type the report
2 my lawyer prepare
3 get their bonuses paid
4 have my hair cut
5 with
6 had two removed
7 we're having
8 by

Page 88

LISTENING

Exercise 1

1 relieved
2 worried
3 surprised
4 disappointed
5 upset
6 tired
7 angry
8 amused

Exercise 2

1 C
2 F
3 B
4 H
5 E

Page 88

SPEAKING

Exercise 1

1 D
2 J
3 J
4 D
5 J
6 D

Exercise 2

Students' own answers

Page 89

USE OF ENGLISH

Exercise 1

1 with
2 by
3 go
4 take
5 get
6 up
7 end
8 off

1 b
2 g
3 e
4 h
5 a
6 d
7 f
8 c

Exercise 2

1 in
2 up
3 over
4 forward
5 round
6 through

Exercise 3

1 b
2 a
3 c
4 d
5 c
6 a
7 d
8 c

Page 90

WRITING

Exercise 1

1 relationship
2 chatty, young people
3 respectful, people in authority

Exercise 2

1 A
2 B
3 B
4 A

Exercise 3

Students' own answers

Page 91

Progress check

Exercise 1

1 c
2 a
3 c
4 b
5 b
6 b
7 c
8 b
9 a
10 b

Exercise 2

1 should
2 can't
3 would
4 must
5 needn't
6 wouldn't
7 should
8 had it repaired
9 by
10 have
11 had
12 painted

Cumulative progress

Exercise 3

1 had
2 such
3 would
4 having
5 could
6 most
7 were
8 if

UNIT 12

Pages 92–93

READING

Exercise 1

1 brave, selfless, dull, trustworthy, heroic
2 scared, unreliable, insecure, bad-tempered, selfish, rebellious

Exercise 2

1 For
2 classic
3 Just

Exercise 3

1 F – The problem with these (heroes is that they are also usually incredibly dull.)
2 F – For example, instead of (being brave they …)
3 F – However, the term itself (was first used in the 17th century.)
4 F – Over 200 films have (been made about him (second only to the character of Sherlock Holmes …)
5 T – He can feel love, (jealousy and anger just like humans.)
6 T – Even modern superheroes seem (to be based on the anti-hero idea.)
7 T – Anti-heroes reflect the world (we live in, a world in which issues are not always black or white, right or wrong and people have their faults.) / … they represent our own journey (through life and the choices we must make.)

Exercise 4

1 d
2 h
3 g
4 a
5 e
6 b
7 f
8 c

Page 94

GRAMMAR 1

Exercise 1

1 b
2 c
3 d
4 a

Exercise 2

1 will have been waiting
2 won't be collecting
3 may have left
4 I'll be studying

Exercise 3

1 will have become
2 won't be working
3 will have been battling
4 will be serving
5 won't have finished
6 will Bob have been running
7 Will you be driving
8 will have been helping

Page 94

VOCABULARY

Exercise 1

1 criticism
2 racism
3 vegetarianism
4 heroism
5 tourism
6 capitalism
7 idealism
8 favouritism

Exercise 2

1 made sense
2 do her duty
3 made … proud
4 make excuses
5 make a difference
6 doing good

Exercise 3

1 polite, kind
2 typical, ordinary
3 unknown, infamous
4 popular, famous
5 likeable, sympathetic

Page 95

GRAMMAR 2

Exercise 1

1 b
2 d
3 f
4 c
5 a
6 e

Exercise 2

1 Suppose
2 found
3 flooded
4 left
5 Did

Exercise 3

1 wish I knew
2 high time he won
3 rather (that) we worked
4 only I could come

Page 96

LISTENING

Exercise 1

1 B
2 C
3 A

Exercise 2

1 A
2 C
3 B
4 A
5 C

Page 96

SPEAKING

Exercise 1

1 Shall we start with this one?
2 So, do we agree on these qualities?
3 What about taking risks?
4 Do you think we should choose courage?
5 Do you agree that our second choice should be confidence?
6 It looks as if we agree on courage.

Exercise 2

courage, putting others first

Exercise 3

Students should tick:
1, 2, 4, 5

Page 97

USE OF ENGLISH

Exercise 1

1 M
2 A
3 A
4 A
5 M
6 M
7 A
8 A
9 M
10 A

Exercise 2

1 was
2 been
3 were
4 be
5 refused
6 doing
7 is
8 have
9 making
10 will

Exercise 3

1 been
2 had
3 sit
4 be
5 was
6 would
7 make
8 will

Page 98

WRITING

Exercise 1

5

Exercise 2

Students should mark the paragraphs to start at these points:

1 Some people believe that politicians …
Sports stars are another popular …
However, I think ordinary people …
In conclusion, while some …
2 therefore, consequently, for this reason

Exercise 3

Students' own answers

Page 99

Progress check

Exercise 1

1 famous, criticism, capitalist, makes, sensitive
2 tourism, ordinary, made, careful
3 idealism, heroism, unknown, do

Exercise 2

1 c
2 b
3 b
4 a
5 c
6 a
7 b
8 c
9 a
10 b

Cumulative progress

Exercise 3

1 heroism
2 terrible
3 unaware
4 Unbelievably
5 strength
6 gradually
7 disability
8 admirable

OPTIMISE Practice test

Page 100

Reading and Use of English

Part 1

1 B
2 A
3 A
4 C
5 A
6 C
7 B
8 D

Part 2

9 where
10 previously/before/ago
11 than
12 Although
13 Both
14 was
15 their
16 be

Part 3

17 behaviour
18 development
19 unreasonable
20 personality
21 relationships
22 happiness
23 relatively
24 disagree

Part 4

25 you mind lending me
26 has never been to
27 if he hadn't / had not been
28 was built by
29 is not warm enough
30 had her bag stolen

Part 5

31 C	**33** B	**35** A
32 D	**34** B	**36** C

Part 6

37 D	**39** F	**41** G
38 A	**40** C	**42** B

Part 7

43 D	**47** B	**51** B
44 C	**48** C	**52** A
45 A	**49** D	
46 C	**50** D	

Page 110

Writing

Part 1

Students' own answers

Part 2

Students' own answers

Page 112

Listening

Part 1

1 B	**3** B	**5** A
2 A	**4** C	

Part 2

6 floods
7 stronger
8 12–15
9 on poles or stilts
10 local builders
11 way of life
12 accommodation
13 twice

Part 3

14 H	**16** F	**18** D
15 A	**17** B	

Part 4

19 B	**21** A	**23** C
20 A	**22** B	

Page 116

Speaking

Part 1

Students' own answers

Part 2

Students' own answers

Part 3

Students' own answers

Part 4

Students' own answers